# Nyima Tashi

Nyima Tashi

# Nyima Tashi

The Songs and Instructions of the
First Traleg Kyabgön Rinpoche

Translated by Yeshe Gyamtso

KTD Publications
Woodstock, New York USA

Published by:
KTD Publications
335 Meads Mountain Road
Woodstock, NY 12498 USA
www.KTDPublications.org

Distributed by:
Namse Bangdzo Bookstore
335 Meads Mountain Road
Woodstock, NY 12498 USA
www.NamseBangdzo.com

ISBN 0-9741092-8-2
This book is printed on acid free paper.

# Contents

The Ninth Traleg Kyabgön Rinpoche
Thrangu Monastery, East Tibet, 2004

# Foreword
## by the Ninth Traleg Kyabgön Rinpoche

Gampopa, the peerless physician from Dakpo, who was repeatedly predicted and praised by the Buddha, caused the teachings of the lineage of accomplishment to become widespread in the Himalayan land of Tibet. All his disciples gave rise to the sudden realization of Mahamudra. Among them were five hundred great meditators, of whom the greatest and most famous were the three Khampas.

One of these three was the Khampa Saltong Shogom, who achieved the greatest mastery of the channels and winds through the practice of chandali. His rebirth was Nyima Tashi the Birth-Recollector, who devoted his life to silent practice in sealed retreat. He saw the faces of yidams, realized Mahamudra, and thereafter recounted his previous births and prophesied his future ones. He sang vajra songs that are still warm with his blessing.

This brief account of his recollections, prophecies of future births, and songs has now been translated into English and published. It is certain that disciples who study it will plant the seed of liberation in their continuums. I therefore rejoice in and am grateful for its publication.

*Written by one called Traleg Tulku on the fifteenth of August, 2005.*

# Translator's Introduction

This book is a translation of a short collection of the songs and teachings of the First Traleg Kyabgön Rinpoche, Nyima Tashi. It is not a biography in the usual sense of the word, and in fact little is known about Nyima Tashi's life. He is said to have lived at the time of Chödrak Gyamtso, the Seventh Gyalwang Karmapa (1454-1505), who is said to have been his guru.

The Traleg Kyabgöns have been principal lineage holders of Thrangu Monastery, a major monastery of the Karma Kagyu tradition in Eastern Tibet, since the sixteenth century. Before then, in fact before the name Traleg Kyabgön was given to this succession of incarnations, this holy being served the Buddha's teachings and demonstrated the achievement of awakening time after time under many names. This book tells us about several of these prior incarnations. In essence, the Traleg Kyabgön is the bodhisattva Vajrapani, the personification of the power of all buddhas. The title "Kyabgön," "Refuge and Protector," is no exaggeration.

Gratitude is due to Traleg Kyabgön Rinpoche for his foreword and for his permission to translate this short book, and to Khenpo Karthar Rinpoche, the abbot of Karma Triyana Dharmachakra Monastery, without whose help and guidance this project, like so many others, would have been impossible.

*Yeshe Gyamtso*

*This translation is dedicated to the*
*Ninth Traleg Kyabgön Rinpoche*

The Peerless Holy Guru Nyima Tashi's
Collected Songs, Instructions, and
Recollections of Previous Lives,
Along with the Story of His Relics

# Songs and Instructions

# Songs and Instructions

Namo Guru.
To Vajradhara, the sixth buddha and lord of all
    families;[1]
To glorious guru Karmapa, indivisible from him;
And to his activity, renowned as Nyima Tashi,[2]
I bow with devotion.
Motivated by bodhichitta, I will set forth here
Merely the smallest particle of the glorious
    mountain
Of his garland of lives, profound and secret,
Born from the splendid ocean of the three
    accumulations.[3]

The glorious guru Nyima Tashi, the guide of the whole
world, the holy source of refuge for the three realms, the
one like a precious wish-fulfilling jewel, the peerless
torch dispelling the darkness of all four continents and
the subcontinents, realized the meaning of emptiness. He

mastered Mahamudra. While remaining for many years in one-pointed, sealed retreat he examined his channels and winds. As a sign of his mastery of the channels, winds, and drops he recollected one hundred and eighty births. He therefore became known as "the one who remembers one hundred and eighty births."

He once wrote, "Many births ago, at the time of the great sage Shakyaraja, Ananda displayed innumerable emana-tions.[4] These included innumerable emanations of Vajrapani. In order to display miracles, Ananda emanat-ed me. At that time I was known as Vajrapani Uchaya Stalk of Secret Mantra."

Beginning with that birth, he extensively described his recollections of each of his lives up to his birth as Nyima Tashi, including astonishing accounts of his assistance to beings and his great compassion. This all comprised an entire wondrous volume. He also wrote an account com-prising slightly more than thirty folios. Unfortunately, a wicked attendant said to him, "Since you never described your great qualities in such detail while your hair was still black, why do it now that your hair is white?"

Nyima Tashi replied, "Oh! You're right!" He then burnt the manuscripts of his accounts in a fire that was ablaze before him. He did this because of that attendant's unfor-tunate remark.

Then the guru thought, "I know that my impermanent body is soon to be destroyed."

He announced, "I will not remain here! It's time for me to go to Sukhavati!"[5]

He then sang this song of impermanence:

> Precious lord, root guru,
> Grant your blessing that renunciation arise in my
>     heart.
>
> The composite things of samsara have no essence.
> They are impermanent, impermanent, without
>     essence.
> Changing, changing, without essence.
> Moving, moving, without essence.
> Destructible, destructible, without essence.
> My story is without essence.
> Samsaric things are without essence.
>
> The external environment changes and is
>     destructible.
> Its inhabitants, sentient beings, also change
>     and are destructible.
> The sun, moon, and stars on high also change
>     and are destructible.
> The earth, mountains, and rocks down below
>     also change and are destructible.
> The southern clouds over the horizon also change
>     and are destructible.
> White, snowy Mount Habo in the highlands also
>     changes and is destructible.
> The blue Tsangpo River in the lowlands also
>     changes and is destructible.
> The mountains, rocks, and trees to our right also
>     change and are destructible.
> The mountains, green fields, and flowers to our
>     left also change and are destructible.

The seasons—summer, winter, fall, and spring—
   also change and are destructible.
Day, night, years, and months also change and
   are destructible.
All such things are expressions of change.

We mundane beings, even if we circle the four
   continents and subcontinents,
Are without essence.
Even if our wealth and possessions increase,
   they are without essence.
Even if we amass armor, weapons, sons, and
   horses, they are without essence.
Even if we gather together our parents and
   relatives, they are without essence.
Even if our happiness and fame are great, they
   are without essence.
Even if we possess power, wealth, and youth,
   they are without essence.

The seats of high gurus change and are
   destructible.
The assembly halls of lowly sanghas also
   change and are destructible.
The power and affluence of monarchs also
   change and are destructible.
Fixation on the permanence of enemies and
   friends also changes and is destructible.
Everything is impermanent, changes, and is
   destructible.

This birth is like summer crops.
This aging is like a necklace of lotuses.

This sickness is like a fish on hot sand.
This death is like dew hit by sunlight.
These friends are like thorns in your bedding.
This wealth is like designs in a rainbow.
This next life is like crops grown from seeds.
These appearances are like an illusory gathering.
This mind is like a clear sky.

There is no essence in any composite.
Especially, there is nothing in the life of beings to
    grasp as permanent.
Do not be distracted by useless activities!
Accomplish useful virtue!

That was what Nyima Tashi sang. Two brothers who were
his nephews said to him, "Don't say that! Please remain
for at least this year!" The guru, however, did not consent
to do so. Instead, he sang this song:

Precious guru with a lineage,
Remain as an inseparable ornament atop my head.
While praying, I'm going.
While resting evenly, I'm going.
While meditating on the profound path, I'm going.
While guarding samaya, I'm going.[6]
While cultivating pure appearances, I'm going.
While taking appearances on the path, I'm going.
Without attachment to places, I'm going.
Without yearning for friends, I'm going.
Without sadness about companions, I'm going.
Without craving for food, I'm going.
Without attachment to wealth, I'm going.
Meditating on my guru from my heart, I'm going.

Shooting out my consciousness like an arrow, I'm
  going.
I will eject it into my father guru's heart!

Because Nyima Tashi sang that song, his nephews said,
"If you will not remain and must go, please bestow instructions on all assembled here." In response, the guru
sang this:

Lord, all buddhas of the three times embodied
  as one,
Beings' protector, glorious and supreme guru,
Kind essence of the three jewels:
I pray that you protect me, lord guru.

Even a seemingly pleasant, pleasant home
Is abandoned and destroyed when away, away
  you go.
Even seemingly loving, loving relatives
Cry in anguish when your breath comes to a
  sudden, sudden stop.

Although nice, nice talk is diverting,
It won't reoccur, reoccur. This hurts us.
Although through this attachment to your
  beautiful, beautiful body
You adorn it with fine, fine jewelry,

When your circulation comes to a harsh, harsh end,
No matter how many loving, loving relatives
  surround you,
You will be caught by terrifying, terrifying Death.
With bulging, bulging eyes you'll gaze at his face.

With a quivering, quivering body you'll wail.

If you don't practice holy dharma immediately,
    immediately,
Your life will be wasted by a distracted, distracted
    mind.
You will be stuck again and again in the box of
    samsara.

Stuck again, again; circling again, again!
Although it seems hard, so hard, apply yourself to
    virtue.
Although it seems miserable, so miserable at the
    time, practice austerity.
Although it's easy, so easy, abandon wrongdoing.

Although it seems like a nice, nice place, abandon
    samsara.
Your head will be covered only by white, white
    hair.
Your frail, frail form will be covered by wrinkles.
Your bent, bent body will lean on a cane.

Your timid, timid mind will be unable to do any-
    thing.
Those things that seemed delightful, so delightful
    at the time,
Will become sources of delight, such delight for
    others.
Shaking, shaking, you'll go alone without the
    ability to take
The slightest, slightest amount of your wealth
    with you.

Again and again think of death in your heart.
Practice divine dharma of certain, certain benefit.
Pray to the guru with a loud, loud voice.
Put everything into anguished, anguished devotion.

Give up plans for successful success in this life.
These vivid, vivid external appearances
Appear to exist, exist, but are like dreams.
These various distinct, distinct sounds
Are loud, loud emptiness like an echo.
In this mind that is aware and aware of various
     things,
Whatever arises and arises is awareness-display
     beyond intellect.
It is good for the mind to search for itself: its
     self-nature.

I have sung these truth-like stanzas of truth,
As they appeared fleetingly, fleetingly in my mind.
If they seem correctly correct, consider them.
If these words are pretty, so pretty, sing them.
If they seem not, not at all, cast them behind you.

Although I see no great, great meaning in
This babbling speech formed like formal verse
I have sung it like the repetitive, repetitive speech
     of a parrot.

Those verses employing duplication were composed
at Garuda Fortress. Nyima Tashi also sang this:

KYE HO!
Listen without distraction, fortunate ones assem-
     bled here!

Whether or not you become free from this abyss,
This great ocean of samsara, depends on what
    you do.
This awful body, this swamp of flesh and blood,
    is nevertheless supreme
If it is a container of the practice of holy dharma.
If it becomes a container of wrongdoing you will
    wander in samsara.

Practice these instructions of the guru that are
    like amrita[7]
As you would treat an illness with medicine.
Don't drink the evil poison of wrong views.
Don't waste this body that you have now.
To waste it is a great tragedy.

It is better to practice the guru's instructions for
    one day
Than to fill Jambudvipa with jewels.
It is better to serve the guru for one day
Than to turn Jambudvipa into a treasury.
It is better to exert your body and speech in
    virtuous practice for one day
Than to fill this world of Jambudvipa with food
    and wealth.

Practice virtue, that which is supreme.
Abandon wrongdoing, that which should be
    avoided like poison.

Take your own body as an example.
You don't need arrows, spears, or swords.
Just pierce your body with a needle.
Look at the extent of your body's pain.

13

The bodies of other sentient beings are just like
    that.

Whatever you do to others you will experience five
    hundred times.
Your suffering through pain will be nine times
    greater.
Therefore take your own body as an example.
Don't harm the bodies of any other beings.
The result of doing so will ripen for you alone.

Men and women of precipitous Kham,[8]
Keep this in mind. This is advice from my heart.
Happy songs are like the call of a skylark: useless!
Keep this in mind.

The wealth and possessions we greedily
    accumulate,
If not used as provisions for the next life, are a
    waste.
Keep this in mind.

If you reach the age of a hundred years without
    practicing holy dharma,
The fifty years worth of days have been spent in
    distraction and bewildered activity.
The fifty years worth of nights have been spent
    in a stupor, lying around like a corpse.
The entire hundred years have been wasted.
Even worse, we scramble to do as much evil as
    we can.
Hold in your compassion those of precipitous
    Kham with evil karma!

We renunciates wearing yellow robes
Are utterly pretentious as we steal and hoard.
We melodiously chant high-sounding jargon while
    ringing our bells.
We arrange beforehand our inheritance of others'
    wealth and possessions.
We cannot bear to use so much as a scrap of food
    offered to us in faith
For virtuous purposes such as the support of
    dharma practice,
The painting of images, or the creation of supports.
We barter it for profit, which is ninefold wrong-
    doing.
The interest we earn on such property is a stem of
    poison.
It would be better if such interest were used to
    support dharma,
Even though it would still be hoarding. Yet we
    don't do even that.
We pour this accumulated wealth into the hands
Of laymen and women called "serfs."
This is planting the stem of poison in a turnip
    field.
Don't do this. It is the wrong way to act.

Once you have enough for your own mouth and
    back,
Give whatever is left to the three jewels.
Others exist besides you. Keep this in mind.

Those accorded the august title "dharmic persons"
    nowadays
Don't tame their own minds; they are as hard
    as nails.

Put effort into taming your crooked mind.
Always meditate on great love and compassion
For all the living and the dead connected to you
    by mouth or hand.

Always bind with the lasso of love and
    compassion
This wild black wind of pride and the five
    poisons.[9]
Quench with the rain of emptiness and
    compassion
Anger's dark red, blazing pit of fire.

Keep all these things in the clear expanse of your
    mind.
Keep them in mind. This is advice from my heart.

These final instructions were taught for renunciates and
for beings in general.

Then Nyima Tashi gave his final instructions, containing
advice for this life and the next, for chieftains, ministers,
leaders, fathers, uncles, sons, mothers, aunts, and
maidens:

EMAHO!
In the vast sky of the view, Mahamudra,
Is the Great Perfection, like a rainbow in that sky.
This mind-in-itself, luminosity that pervades all
    samsara and nirvana,
Is like a never-setting sun without fluctuation in
    its brilliance.

I salute and praise the precious Kagyu.
I, Nyima Tashi, the culmination of the awareness

Embodied in Saltong Shogom's series of births,[10]
See clearly in the state of dharmakaya[11]
Whatever arises in your minds, good or bad.
Let your minds not be lost in doubt, worthy
    disciples. Listen.

In these evil dregs of time renunciates and
    laypeople, the powerful and the weak,
All the men and women in the whole country,
Fail to know their place. Their ambitions are
    sky-high.
Don't be like that. It's the wrong way to act.

All of us gathered here, both men and women,
Are getting closer and closer to death with the
    passing of each year,
Closer and closer to death with the passing of
    each month,
Closer and closer to death with the passing of
    each day.

Men and women in this abyss of samsara,
There is no time to do lots of good and evil.
Even if you do a lot, it is self-deception.
Don't do a lot. Think about dharma.
After this life there will be the next. Keep this in
    mind.

On the road out of this life
None of your family will be of the slightest help.
They will hurt you.
They will weep torrential tears of blood.
They will drive you over a precipice with their
    crying.

Survivors of the dying,
Don't cry and rain down torrents of tears.
All sentient beings, high and low,
Lose their physical bodies to impermanence.
What good is a lot of crying then?
All this wailing and crying
Causes the dying to become more attached
    and bewildered.
The sound of loud crying is no help.
It can cause the dying to fall into hell.
Don't wail and cry.
All you men and women, high and low,
Keep this in mind.

The three realms are impermanent, like clouds
    in the sky, are they not?
The four seasons are impermanent.
The withered and the green both change.
Summer and winter both change.
During the three months of summer and the
    three of fall
The earth's warmth overcomes the cold wind.
The trees, forests, and flowers are very colorful.
During the three months of winter and the three
    of spring
The earth's warmth disappears.
The trees and forests, being impermanent, change.
The elements are destroyed.
Look at the changing of the seasons.
Our bodies are also impermanent.
Don't take what is impermanent to be permanent.

All of us gathered here, high and low,

Have acquired the leisure and resources of this
    human body.
If we are unable to at least not waste it entirely,
A greeting party from hell will await us
On the road out of this life.

The results of virtue and wrongdoing ripen
    individually.
Most of the teachings of the many buddhas of the
    past
And most of the many stories we hear
Are about distinguishing between right and wrong.

The suffering in the hot and cold hells is great.
The edges of the awful weapons there are sharp.

Those of us who are very greedy now
Will be born in the preta realm after death.[12]
The suffering there from hunger and thirst is
    immeasurable.

Those of us who bear great hatred toward other
    lands
Will be born in the asura realm after death.
The suffering there from fighting and quarrelling
    is immeasurable.

Those of us who continually slaughter animals
Will be born immediately after death in a cauldron
    in hell.
We will hear shouts of "Kill, kill!" and "Beat,
    beat!"
For many years we will suffer being cooked,
    roasted, and burnt.

We will wail in the unbearable suffering of heat
  and cold.
We will cry tears of blood.
Laypeople gathered here,
Don't slaughter many animals!
You will be tormented in the cauldrons of hell.

Marriage is impermanent, like clouds in the sky.
Don't fight and quarrel too much.
Doing so will also cause rebirth in the place of
  fighting.

Life is impermanent, like a flash of lightning in
  the sky.
Thinking life is long, we burden ourselves with
  wrongdoing.
Not accomplishing holy dharma, we accomplish
  hell for ourselves.
To achieve one's own ruin is pathetic.

Wealth and possessions are impermanent, like dew
  on a blade of grass.
There is no certainty as to when it will be suddenly
  destroyed by the sun.
Earnestly offer and give in accordance with what
  you have.
Possessions are impermanent, like acquisition in
  a dream.
As soon as you awake it all vanishes like a rainbow.
Everything is impermanent in that same way.
Those who take the impermanent to be permanent
Are deceiving themselves.

We hustle to engage in as much wrongdoing

as we can
By slaughtering, plowing, and grinding.
This is like knowingly swallowing deadly poison.
It is like intentionally drowning yourself.

All of us gathered here have acquired human
  bodies.
If we don't practice holy dharma in this body
There is only one chance in a hundred
That we'll acquire a human body again.

Will we or won't we? Look at all who live in this
  land.
Look up at the great mountains.
How many wild animals do you see?
How many human beings do you see?
Think about whether you will acquire a human
  body or not.

Look at the interior of a great land
Or the center of a vast field.
Consider the ratio of four-legged animals to
  humans.
That will make the rarity of human bodies clear.

Look between blades of grass in a field
During the three months of summer and the three
  of fall.
Look at whether there are more people or more
  bugs.
The bugs are a rushing mass of pallid life.
Because bad karma is so common their inferior
  bodies are so numerous.
In comparison, human beings are few.

Think about this. You will understand the rarity of
　　the human body.

How many birds do you see in the sky?
Look at the spectacle of life in a river.
Because of bad karma, fish, frogs, tadpoles, and
　　waterfowl abound.
These innumerable animals are foolish and
　　bewildered.
The number of animals, all unable to speak, is
　　inconceivable.
How many human beings, those able to speak,
　　do you see?
Using your water-bubble eyes look at which is
　　greater,
The number of fortunate humans or the number
　　of unfortunate animals.

All the variety displayed in space is created
By a little child called All-Doing King.[13]
This little child, lucidity-emptiness, like a lamp,
Lives in the heart, that mansion of flesh
That lies on the anthers on top of this two-legged
　　tree.

His play is the variety of whatever arises.
Ask him whether the leisure and resources of
　　this human body are rare or not.
He won't answer the first time you ask,
But if you ask repeatedly he has advice to give.

This child, awareness, All-Doing King,
Because he is a child, mistakes himself for a self.
Because he is not just a child,

He is the ground of all samsara and nirvana.

At this one time when you have acquired
The leisure and resources of a human body
Avoid the wrongdoing of a distracted life.
It is pitiful not to practice the holy dharma
    beneficial in the future
And thereby pass to a lower state at death.

Therefore look. Look at your mind.
This mind-in-itself has no substantial existence.
Look at its nature, free of existence.
These various appearances are the miraculous
    display of that nature.

These miracles arise from that nature.
These miracles dissolve into that nature.
Like the moon's reflection in water,
There is no apprehended and no apprehender
In emptiness without any substantial existence.

There is nothing of which to be mindful,
No one to be mindful,
And no place to put the mind.
Although there is no place to put it and no one to
    do so,
When there is mindfulness there is immaculate
    clarity.
This is the nature of all things.

Whatever arises, good or bad, look at its nature.
Whatever arises, don't alter or change it.
Rest in freshness, freedom from alteration.
The samadhi of resting in just-that, without
    alteration, is Mahamudra.

The victors have said
That there is no need to doubt whether it is or not.

Abandon hope for progress and fear of faults.
If you continuously foster with mindfulness
All the variety of awareness, thought, and mental
     activity,
Whatever arises is self-liberated great bliss.

It is more meritorious to meditate on emptiness
     for a single session
Than to accumulate defiled virtue for a kalpa.
Although there are innumerable imputed gates
     of dharma devised by the intellect,
If the nature's true face is unrealized they are of
     little meaning.

Therefore, those among you who wish in your
     hearts to practice holy dharma,
Don't gaze at spectacles. Gaze at your mind.
Don't clean your body. Clean your mind.

Look at external appearances.
These appearances are ungraspable emptiness.
When looked at they are not seen. Rest relaxed
     in their nature.

When you rest your mind it doesn't remain still.
Without legs, it nevertheless roams the four
     continents.
Look at that which roams about.
It doesn't go far. It naturally returns to you.
For example, golden-eyed fish are not still.
They roam all over the ocean's depths.

Yet they don't really go far.
They never leave the ocean itself.

Look at the nature of your inner awareness.
Look at what this All-Doing King is doing.
He has a lot to do.
All the various positive qualities come from him.
He is also the source of all flaws.
Self-awareness is the sole root of everything.

Knowing this, emptiness and compassion will be
    united.
With unfabricated, spontaneous, great compassion
    for all unrealized beings,
Affix the seal of triple purity—
Not conceptualizing dedicated virtue, its dedicator,
    or its dedication.
This is the basis of supreme, unsurpassable
    awakening.

Appearances, sounds, and thoughts have been the
    dharmakaya from the beginning.
If you know that and are without fixation on them,
There is nothing to be done to the appearances of
    the six groups.
Self-liberated in that state of relaxation, they are
    great bliss, the dharmakaya.
This is the unsurpassable wisdom of all buddhas.
It is the entire point of all dharma.

Human life is impermanent, like a butter lamp
    in the wind.
The Mara of Death awaits the onset of shadow.[14]
We are impermanent, like the setting sun.

Wealth is impermanent, like dew on grass.
Possessions are impermanent, like clouds in
    the sky.
Marriages are impermanent, like the meeting
    of shoppers at a marketplace.

Yama's messengers strike like lightning.[15]
The obstacles of Mara are as sudden as an
    earthquake.

You people of the world, listen.
Fearing the cold, we cover with animal skins
This impure, illusory body; this aggregate of flesh
    and blood;
This decrepit, bloody mansion; this body of
    magical illusion.
We weave colorful silk for it from bugs' slime.
We look at ourselves and ask, "Do I look nice?"

Fearing hunger, we sustain our vigor with food.
We cook it in all sorts of ways, asking "Is it
    delicious? Is it appealing?"
To make it delicious, we add everything other
    than earth and stones.
Such is the food we consume in order to feed
    ourselves.

This body, covered without and fed within,
Is illusory, a house of flesh and blood.
As with any ruin, you never know when it's going
    to fall down.

Be vigorous in dharma starting from today.
Those of you who have been accomplishing
    wrongdoing and not holy dharma,

Turn your thoughts to dharma starting from today.
You don't know when the Mara of Death will
    come for you.
Turn your thoughts to dharma starting from today.
You don't know when the bandits, Yama's messen-
    gers, will arrive.
Turn your thoughts to dharma starting from today.
You don't know when your illusory body will be
    struck by illness.
Turn your thoughts to dharma starting from today.
You don't know when, struck by illness, this body
    will be destroyed.
Turn your thoughts to dharma starting from today.
You don't know when spirits will suddenly attack
    your body.
Turn your thoughts to dharma starting from today.
At death you will experience the suffering of the
    six states.
Turn your thoughts to dharma starting from today.
The suffering in each of the six states is
    unimaginable.
Turn your thoughts to dharma starting from today.

Chieftains of great communities,
Make holy dharma the basis of your rule.
Think about this: There are both this and future
    lives.
Don't attract curses by ruling unjustly.
If you do, women will curse you in rage.
In this life various misfortunes will occur.
Worse things than that will occur in the next.
If your rule is dharmic, this in itself is going for
    refuge.

Think about this: There are both this and future
     lives.

Outer and inner ministers, and chieftains' sons,
You frequently say that the chieftain said things he
     didn't.
You bring immeasurable pain and suffering to your
     community.
Once you say yes or no, there is no opportunity
     for argument.
You snap your whip and drive in your spurs.
When you return to the chieftain,
You report that the people said many things they
     didn't.
Angering the chieftain, you bring misery on the
     community.
Don't do these things, chieftains' sons and tax
     collectors.
It is said to be more dangerous to be cursed by the
     people
Than to be held in enmity by many Buddhist and
     Bönpo magicians.
The curses of many enraged women can make a
     landslide of vajra rock
Or dry up a great ocean.
There is danger of being struck by unhappiness,
Suffering, and great sickness. Don't do these
     things.
In the next life you will suffer greatly in hell.
You will be born in a place where you will be
     cooked and burnt
For an entire life lasting trillions of years.
Don't do these things. Turn your mind to dharma.

Holy dharma has great blessing.

Old fathers and uncles from all the land,
Don't carry the burden of bad habits in your minds.
Carry holy dharma, helpful later on, in your minds.
Don't choose the wrong burden.
If you do, you'll be lost in this life and the next.
You are obeyed, fed, and served far beyond your
    needs
By your sons, your nephews, and your whole
    families.
One day, however, an obstacle will descend on
    you as suddenly as lightning.
Your offspring will be of no help.
Aside from a few good, dharmic persons,
People are not helpful to the dead in these evil
    days.
A few good, dharmic persons
Will remember your face and mourn you.
Their sincere grief will inspire them to engage in
    virtue.
People like that, however, are rarer than daytime
    stars.
Most people will have forgotten you three days
    after your death.
If you doubt this, look at how those already dead
    are treated.
You will wander, alone and sad, in the terrifying
    interval,
The land of Yama.
None of your friends or family will accompany you.
None of your sons or nephews will accompany you.
Through the power of karma,

The results of your virtuous and evil deeds will
    await you.
The minions of Death will chase you.
There will be no place to hide even your killing of
    a single louse.
Now, when you have acquired the leisure and
    resources of this human body,
Exert yourselves in virtue, sons of family.

Old mothers and aunts who have crossed the pass
    of life,
Don't follow the five poisons and attachment.
You are quite capable of deception.
Your mouths are treasuries of wrongdoing.
You are as busy as demons.
If out of great desire you cast monks' vows into
    the dirt,
You will be born on Shalma Mountain where
    desire is burnt up
And remain there for thousands of years.[16]
You will suffer immeasurably.
All kinds of physical, verbal, and mental wrong-
    doing are there in your minds.
Great desire is there in your minds.
Great hatred is there in your minds.
Great stupidity is there in your minds.
Great pride is there in your minds.
Great jealousy is there in your minds.
Great greed is there in your minds.
Vanity and acquisitiveness are there in your minds.
The five poisonous afflictions are all there in your
    minds.
You unfortunate women!

You repeat whatever you hear.
You apply yourselves to whatever you think of.
You eat whatever you find.
You rush off to do whatever occurs to you.
Your wagging tongues can agitate an entire
    country
When for no reason you bring up in conversation
Things no one wants to talk about.
For no reason you curse those committed to virtue.
Women stuck in home life, don't be like that!

Old men and women from all the land,
Think how many years you have lived.
Consider how many people your age have died.
Think how close you are to death.
Don't aggravate or obstruct
The younger members of your households.
Practice whatever divine dharma you can.
Repeat the six syllables with your mouths.[17]
Turn mani wheels with your hands.
Meditate seriously on death and impermanence
    in your minds.
Consider how many relatives of your age
Remain and how many have died.
We are bewildered in taking the impermanent
    to be permanent.
Old people, eradicate bewilderment.
Old people, cultivate impartial pure perception.
Old people, meditate on death from your hearts.
Old people, meditate on your guru above your
    head.
Look up at this evening sun.
Is it closer to rising or setting?

Old, bewildered people, think about it.
The impermanence of old age is like the setting
    sun.
Old men and women, this is advice from my
    heart.
We have no assurance as to when the Mara of
    Death will come.
He makes no distinction between old and young.
Exert yourselves in divine dharma from the heart.
Keep this in mind. It is advice from my heart.

Listen once more, patron Sönam Pel,
Son of the dharma lineage of Gompa Dorje.[18]
Sönam Pel, descendant of Ralpa Kambep,
Don't get lost in the wrong path of action.
Practice holy dharma!

That was what Nyima Tashi sang. The patron Sönam Pel
then said, "Although I've accumulated quite a bit of
wealth, it is meaningless. My only son is an idiot inca-
pable of any work. I am sad. I think I should use my
wealth to support holy dharma. It was very kind of you to
sing us old men and women those songs and instructions
concerning impermanence. I now intend to use my
wealth to sponsor paintings of deities and the copying of
scriptures. What dharma should be copied? Also, please
bestow upon the young men and women here their share
of dharma. Please don't leave them out!" In response, the
guru sang this:

Listen once more, descendant of Ralpa Kambep.
The paintings and scriptures you sponsor should
    be these:

It would be good to paint the twelve deeds.[19]
Then have whatever sutras you wish copied.


Young men and women gathered here,
Men and women in the bloom of youth,
Don't view your old parents as demons.
If you see these three—parents, gurus, and
     teachers—
As demons and give rise to wrong views,
You will be born in the hell of ceaseless torment.
Calling it yours, you make as much profit as
     you can
On the wealth accumulated by your parents
     and ancestors.
You then throw into the garbage, like a rotten hide,
The parents who first accumulated that wealth.
You falsely claim to have earned the wealth
     yourself.
Your parents, the people who really accumulated
     the wealth,
Look up at what you do from the garbage pit.
At the first sign of them questioning your actions,
You say, "Old dogs, old corpses, I can't understand
     your muttering!"
You call them all sorts of awful names.
You will be born five hundred times with the awful
     body
Of whatever you have called
Your kind parents, gurus, or teachers.
In between you will experience many sufferings
     in the hells.
Young men and women, don't do those things.

It has been said by the victors that kind parents,
    gurus, and teachers
Are objects of veneration.
Men and women in the bloom of youth,
I could say much more but you wouldn't under-
    stand.
This drop of advice from my heart about holy
    dharma
Is unlike any mundane conversation.
It is exactly what is taught in all sutras and tantras.
However, since worldly men and women in this
    age of degeneracy
Cannot understand them, I have placed my advice
    in a mundane context.
If anything I have said is untrue, I apologize.

All worldly people act as though they will never
    die,
As though there is no place called "the interval,"
As though there is no place called "hell,"
As though there are no results to actions called
    "virtue and wrongdoing,"
As though there is no king called Yama
    Dharmaraja,
As though he has no ministers called "henchmen,"
As though they possess no weapons called "blades
    and spears,"
As though there is no great field called "molten
    iron,"
As though there is no precipice called "the pass of
    the dead,"
As though there is no large place called "the field
    of the dead,"

As though there is no terribly hot place called "the
     hot hells,"
As though there is no terribly cold place called
     "the cold hells,"
As though there is no hell called Black Line,
As though there is no hell called Crushing,
As though there is no little house called "house of
     iron,"
As though there are no cauldrons in hell in which
     to be cooked,
As though there is no boiling, molten iron.

Sentient beings with bad karma, wandering
     through the interval,
Are bound and dragged by the throat with lassos
     made of black snakes.
Amidst thunder, lightning, hail, and torrential rain,
They are without freedom, naked, with empty
     hands.
Yet people act as though they will never have to go
     there,
As though they will live forever in their present
     homes.

How bewildered, how bewildered, how bewil-
     dered are the worldly!
How miserable, how miserable, how miserable are
     the worldly!
If you think about it, they are both miserable and
     bewildered.
Yet they don't know it. Worldly people are mad!
They are worse than mad; they are suicidal!
Unbearable suffering awaits them in the eighteen
     hells.[20]

They cast themselves from here into such a place.

Now, while they live in this world,
We don't see them kill themselves.
However, through the power of their karma,
As soon as they separate from their present bodies
They will bring about their own destruction
Through the ferocious power of ripening karma.

There is no need for doubt as to whether or not
    such things exist.
Understand this, faithful gathered here.
May the guru's blessing enter your hearts.

# Prophecy

# Prophecy

In response to that song, the disciples said, "Holy one, you know everything in the three times. For the benefit of beings in the future, please bestow a brief prophecy." The guru sang:

> You the fortunate, listen once more.
> On the tenth day of the last Monkey month,
> While I was immersed in the clear light,
> A silk-like band of five-colored rainbow light
> Appeared from the palace atop the Glorious
>     Copper-Colored Mountain.[21]
>
> In my experience, the mirror of the dharmakaya,
> This light extended toward me like an unfurled silk
>     ribbon.
> On the anthers of a thousand-petalled lotus,
>     amidst rainbow light,
> Appeared a white HRIH blazing with light.

It was as bright as a hundred thousand suns.

I considered whether this was a hallucination or a
    dream.
When I directed my undistracted awareness to it
    for a moment,
It immediately became Padmasambhava
Surrounded by a retinue of male and female
    vidyadharas.
In my vision, he spoke these prophecies:

"Listen without distraction, siddha vajra-holder!
In the evil, degenerate time of thirty-year life spans
There will not be a moment's happiness for Central
    and Eastern Tibet.
Year by year, sickness, warfare, and famine will
    increase
Like a snowstorm turning into a blizzard.

"Many beings will be tormented by famine.
Many different contagious diseases will appear.
Happiness will become impossible for the Tibetan
    people.

"Bönpos and Buddhists will quarrel, denigrating
    and attacking one another.
This will herald war in Central and Eastern Tibet.
The bodhisattvas abiding on the levels
Who live in this land will be cast aside.

"Spirits will enter from outside; people will venerate
    false monks.
This will herald the degeneration of the doctrine
    in Tibet.

Worldly men and women will abandon the virtuous lamas of their locality,
Thinking them as lowly as dogs.

"Outsiders will wander the land. A few liars will
appear.
They will distort much profound dharma,
Saying, 'I do not speak for the sake of illusory
wealth.' [22]
False monks saying that will become accepted as
pure.
They will be held in high esteem.
This will be a further sign of the degeneration of
the doctrine in Tibet.

"The daughter of the great nyen Tanglha in the
North
Will be taken to wife by the drala Pehar the
King.[23]
Her price and reception will be sickness and
warfare.
Many beings will suffer.

"Gods and spirits will flourish then.
Those nonhumans with broken samaya
Will cause agitation in the temples and assemblies
of the sangha.
Tongues will wag with rumors that appear from
nowhere.

"Fighting, feuds, suicidal behavior, and fear will
spread,
Obstructing benevolent aspirations and words
of truth.

At that time I, Padmasambhava, will protect you.

"When the emanation of Great Compassion named
    Manga[24]
Passes from this realm to Akanishtha,
The samaya-corruptor Red Kala will ride a human
    being.[25]
The doctrine of Tibet will be assailed from within
    Ngari.
Many life-trees of the Buddha's doctrine will be
    cut down
By this emanation of Girtika.

"In each of her pores will reside an emanated
    mara-minister.
Each of them will produce a thousand emanations,
    filling all Tibet.
Some, in the guise of spiritual friends, will
    disarrange the sutras and tantras.
Some, in the guise of monarchs, will agitate all
    Tibet.
Some, in the guise of leaders, will agitate their
    areas.
Some, in the guise of ministers, will agitate the
    people.
Some, in the guise of common people, will agitate
    their clans.
Some, in the guise of monks, will agitate
    monasteries.
Some, in the guise of students, will agitate colleges.
Some, in the guise of children, will agitate towns.
Some, in the guise of women, will agitate the two
    communities.[26]

In that way all sorts of misfortune and strife will
    occur.
Those emanations are the doctrine-destroying
    body hair of Mara.

"This red emanation of Mara will ride a human
    being.
In her hands she will hold sharp weapons of fire.
She will lead behind her black dogs of unpleasant
    appearance,
Barking three times unpleasantly.

"The heart of this demonic emanation Kala will
    burst open.
The heart's blood that spills forth
Will form a pool in the ground.
Many people speaking different languages will die
    violently.

"Killers and the ghosts of the killed will fill all Tibet.
A fierce wind of sickness and famine
Will fill all Tibet with thick darkness.
Many beings will die prematurely.

"Blighted harvests, frost, hail, and other disasters
Will blow about like the wind.
Various misfortunes will occur for all people.

"When such evil times appear
Humans and beasts will die from sudden obstacles
Until their corpses are as numerous as stones on
    a path.
With every step that is taken another being will die.
People on both sides of the conflict will exclaim

'What is happening to us?'
It will be nothing other than the murderous spirits
Created by warfare throughout the land,
Spirits caused by fighting between two sides.

"The poisonous heart's fat of earth-lords will spill
    forth.
Enraged, they will spread contagious sickness
    throughout their regions.
People will have purchased their own sickness,
But they will say, 'Why are we dying?
Why are we losing? Why are we ruined?'
These things will happen to all, not just to one."

I asked him, "What will be the best way to stop
    all this?"

He replied, "Recite the Buddha's teachings as
    much as possible.
They are like gold.
If renunciates with the three vows recite them
It is three or four times as effective.[27]
Engage in means of protection in accordance with
    local customs.

"In every treasure that I have concealed is a sad-
    hana of the Wrathful Guru.
These are the outer, inner, and secret sadhanas of
    me, Padma,
In the fierce form of the Guru Heruka with a
    retinue of blazing deities.
Repeatedly perform forceful reversal with great,
    red tormas.[28]

"Especially, in a hidden valley in the West of this
    region
Is a white rock like a conch-colored lion leaping
    into space.
In such a place is the quintessence of my treasures.
You are the karmic inheritor of that dharma.[29]

"In bad, degenerate times it is difficult to arrange
    interdependence.
If, however, the interdependence occurs,
Those treasures are the essence of all my treasures.
The profound quintessence of secret mantra,
Those treasures will cause immeasurable benefit
    to beings
Throughout all directions and time.

"If there are no obstacles to interdependence
For the treasure-revealer named Vajra,
Those concealed, secret treasures will benefit
    beings greatly
And reverse the evil of the times.

"They can reverse emptiness and herukas.
There is no reversal like that elsewhere in the
    world.
Evil will be reversed from the top of a fiery Mount
    Meru.
You are the karmic inheritor of such dharma.

"Because the obstacles are great it will be hard to
    help beings.
Perform, therefore, the reversal of the wrathful
    victors,

Such as the Eight Dispensations, the Wisdom
    Assembly, and Vajrakila.[30]
Perform the outer, inner, and secret sadhanas of
    the Wrathful Guru from all the treasures.

"The torma reversals and exhortation rituals of the
    Wrathful Guru,
Of the red and black forms of Manjushri
    Yamantaka,
Of the red and black forms of Hayagriva, of
    Vajrapani,
And of Krodhakali, Singhamukha, and other
    mother tantras—
I have composed all of these.[31]
There is no doubt that evil will be reversed by
    them.

"It will be reversed by the continuous repetition
Of the SIDDHI mantra throughout many days and
    nights.[32]

"It will be reversed by the holy dharma of the Great
    Perfection,
By the great mother Prajnaparamita,
By the forceful torma reversal of the blazing
    wrathful victors,
By a set of one hundred thousand reversals,
By reversal from the peak of Mount Meru,
By ten thousand recitations of the Heart Sutra,
By a thousand Ushnishavijaya reversals,[33]
By a hundred thousand PADME reversals,[34]
And by the planting of great SIDDHI prayer flags in
    the four directions.
There is no doubt that obstacles of year and month

will be reversed.
These are all in the service of human men and
    women.

"In the service of four-legged animals,
    Generously give gifts to the earth-lords, a hundred
        thousand tormas,
    Cleansing smoke, pacifying white tormas for lords
        of place,
    And a hundred thousand ransom replicas.
    It would be good to recite a thousand water-torma
        offerings,
    Including wealth dharanis and the protection of
        prosperity by White Umbrella.[35]

"Listen once more, siddha vajra-holder!
I, Padma, do not deceive future generations.

"Dampa Sangye of India and Machik Lapdrön
Of Zangri Karmar, through shared aspirations,
Combined their benefit of beings.[36]
In their perfection of awareness-display
They resolved the ground of the mind itself.
There arose the feast of severance
That cuts off samsara at the root.
There arose the feast of severance
That cuts through to the nature of the mind itself.
There arose the feast of severance
That cuts through thoughts of grasped and grasper.
There arose the feast of severance
That cuts through the root of grasping at a self.
There arose the feast of severance
That resolves the equality of friends and enemies.
There arose the feast of severance

That cuts through the appearance of pleasure and
    pain.
There arose the feast of severance
That cuts through thoughts of clean and dirty.
There arose the feast of severance
That cuts through to the equality of hope and fear.
There arose the feast of severance
That resolves that gods and spirits are one's own
    mind.
There arose the feast of severance
That cuts through to the nature of one's own mind.
There is nothing more profound for reversing
    adversity for all beings
Than this great ganachakra of severance.

"Listen once more, siddha vajra-holder!
To reverse adversity for beings in bad, degenerate
    times,
Buddhists can reverse it with the great Kabar
    ceremony.[37]
Bönpos can reverse it with the play of the great
    wrathful ones.
Adversity will be fully reversed by offering one
    hundred and thirty-five
Great white tormas to the viras and dakinis.
It will be reversed by large assemblies loudly
    reciting the twelve branches
Of the Buddha's holy speech.[38]
You will be happy in that life
And achieve awakening in the next.
There is no doubt of this, fortunate son of family.
The Victor's dictates are undeceiving.

"As severance is an offering,

It pleases the gurus and yidams.
Blessings and siddhis fall like rain.

"As severance is generosity,
It satisfies gods, spirits, demons, and obstructors.
Past karma, present conditions, and debts will be
    removed.

"As severance is peaceful,
It pacifies everything in its own place.
As severance is compassion,
It endows all with happiness.

"As severance is forceful,
It obliterates enemies and obstructors.
As severance is absolute truth,
Realization will appear from within.

"As severance is liberation upon arising,
Awareness is liberated in its own place.
As severance is immediate,
The nature is clearly seen.

"As severance is naked,
It is not covered by obscurations.
As severance is unstoppable,
You fly in the sky of miracles.

"As severance is a sword,
It is sharp and hard.
As severance is an axe,
It has a cutting edge.

"As severance is a razor,
Nothing can impede it.

As severance is a dispensation,
It is a supplication of the four lineages.[39]

"As severance is holy dharma,
It is Mahamudra.
As severance is perfect completeness,
Awareness is perfectly complete in the arising of
   anything.

"As severance is the result,
You pass through the remaining paths and stages.
Son, there is no doubt that it will reverse
   obstacles.

"As severance is emptiness,
Adversity is empty in its own place.
As severance is equal flavor,
Ill omens are liberated in their own place.

"As severance is illusion,
Emptiness and miracles are unified.
As severance is a mass of fire,
It burns up a billion worlds.

"As severance is a vajra,
It is the vajra tent of one's own mind.
As severance is a weapon,
It completely cuts through enemies and
   obstructors.

"As severance is all-pervasive,
It fills all samsara and nirvana.
As severance is single,
It fills a billion worlds with miracles all at once.

"As severance is a deity,
 The yidam arises in one's mind.
 As severance is a demon,
 Emptiness is killed by emptiness.

"As severance is the ejection of consciousness,
 One is immediately liberated.

"These are not separate things.
 Everything is complete within this one thing.
 Therefore severance is the Great Perfection.
 There is nothing incomplete or imperfect within it.
 The eighteen emptinesses are complete in it."[40]

When the master had said all this to me I prayed
      to him, saying,
"You have been very compassionate in granting me
      these prophecies.
 Please hold the beings of this degenerate kalpa in
      your compassion.
 Please hold me, an apparent monk who consumes
      the sangha's wealth,
 In your compassion."

In reply, the great master said this:
"EMAHO! Listen once more, siddha vajra-holder!
 From here you will go to the realm of
      Akanishtha.[41]
 For three years you will remain in Sukhavati,
 Attending the protector Amitabha.

"At that time your skull will remain here as a relic.
 Let it be preserved in one piece.

It will possess the ornaments of the Mansion of
    Complete Victory.[42]
These deities will appear on the outside and inside
Of this vast palace of conch:

"The principal image will be Samantabhadra
    Amitabha.
In front of him will be the buddha Vairochana;
In the east, Vajrasattva; in the south,
    Ratnasambhava;
In the west, Amitabha; and in the north,
    Amoghasiddhi.

"The thousand buddhas of this fortunate kalpa,
    the eight mahasiddhas,
And the lineage gurus such as the victor
    Vajradhara
Will be gathered like rain-clouds.
The gurus of all lineages will be there,
Including those of Mahamudra, the path and
    result,
The Great Perfection, the middle way, and
    pacification.

"It is certain that Chakrasamvara, Hevajra,
    Guhyasamaja,
Red Yamantaka, Vajrabhairava,
And all the deities of the four tantras without
    exception
Will be there with their retinues.

"Innumerable other deities and relics will appear.
The buddhas of the ten directions and you are
    indivisible.

That is why all this will appear on your skull.
The yidam deities and you are indivisible.
The dharma protectors and guardians and you
    are never separated.
That is why all this will appear in your relics.

"Advise the people of all Tibet of this.
Those deities will appear on your skull.
If they don't, I, Padma, have deceived you.
There is no doubt, siddha vajra-holder.

"The doubt that arises in your mind
Appears to me in the clear light of the dhar-
    makaya.
Don't doubt! Advise Tibet of this.
Your relics will benefit the beings of Tibet.

"My son, there is no doubt that all human beings
Who come into contact with your skull,
Whether they are alive or dead at the time,
Will be protected in that life and quickly achieve
The path to awakening in the next.

"Great benefit will come from prostration and
    circumambulation.
The number of circumambulations is twenty-five
    hundred.
The number of prostrations is fifty-five hundred."

In response I said to him,
"While I am serving in Sukhavati for three years,
My benefit for beings in Tibet will be interrupted.
At that time all the Tibetan people, obscured by
    misappropriation,

Will say, 'He won't come back!'
They will greatly disparage me.

"Although this causes me no displeasure,
Such evil rumor circulating among all worldly
    people,
Even though it is typical of evil times,
Will be a cause of beings' accumulation of
    bad karma.
Guru, I pray that you consider this with
    compassion.

"When the doctrine of male and female samaya-
    corruptors flourishes,
Comets will appear in a sky the color of blood.
Planetary sickness will flash like lightning
    through the air.
The earth will be ablaze with tumors and
    inflammation.

"Lightning, hail, and strokes will blow about like
    the wind.
The mist of sickness will be circulated by the
    tornadoes of spirits.
Because the matrikas are agitated a poisonous,
    black wind will blow.[43]

"During that time of sickness, famine, and war,
The contagious blood-diseases of the matrikas
    and dakinis
Will cause beings to die suddenly.
Earthquakes, tornadoes, and rains of stone will
    occur.

"Rivers will reverse their courses, burst their banks,
    and flood dry land.
The earth will split apart. Rocks will be shattered.
The mountains and valleys will be filled with
    thieves.
Assassins, brigands, and scoundrels will wander
Through the passes and valleys.

"Painful illnesses will strike everyone like lightning.
At that time, hold beings in your compassion.
Guru Rinpoche, don't be uncompassionate.
In degenerate times, hold all beings in your
    compassion."

I said that to Guru Rinpoche. Guru Padma
    answered,
"EMAHO! Listen once more, wise siddha,
Nirmanakaya of Saltong, named Surya!44

"Many births ago, you were Vajrapani,
Emanated by Ananda.
Possessing the light of boundless emanation,
You served as Vajradhara's attendant.

"After casting aside that body, that awareness
    became
The attendant of Saraha, Nagarjuna, and others.
Possessing unstoppable miraculous abilities,
He was renowned as Unimpeded Light.45

"You then became Dakpa Sherab,
Who attended the mahasiddha Tilopa.
You then became Drogön Lotsa,

Who attended the great Naropa.

"You then became Ngokchen Chöku Dorje,
Who attended the mahasiddha Marpa.
That awareness then became Rechungpa,
Who attended the mahasiddha Mila.

"That awareness then became Saltongpa,
Who attended Daö Shönnu.[46]
You then became Ngagi Wangchuk,
Who appeared in India as a pandit.

"After his nirvana you became Trakchuk,
Who possessed the discipline of wild behavior.[47]
He attended Rangjung Dorje.
That awareness then became a monk named
    Chökyi Wangchuk
Who benefited many disciples and led many
    beings
To the path of awakening.

"That awareness was then born at Karma,
And became a monk named Karma Chöwang.
He attended the protector of beings;[48]
Created many supreme supports of body, speech,
    and mind;
And established many beings on the path to
    liberation.

"His emanation was called Sangye Tendzin.
He served the Buddha's doctrine at Tago.
Your next birth was called Sönam Tashi.
Benefiting beings through dharma, he fulfilled
    the hopes of disciples.

"After that you became the supreme scholar
    Sherab Gyamtso,
Who impartially served all the Buddha's doctrine.
His emanation was the supreme lord of siddhas,
Kunga Sönam, the protector of beings.
The next emanation was named Döndrup and
    tamed beings.

"You, Nyima Tashi, are his emanated light.
You will benefit beings for seven more lives.
While engaged in your future benefit of beings,
The name 'Nyima' will never change.[49]

"Then, after your parinirvana in that life,
You will become a renowned treasure-revealer
    named Dorje.[50]
At that time you will embody the discipline of
    diverse emanation.
You will have a birthmark on your back
And distinct svastikas on your feet.

"You will reveal innumerable treasure dharmas
That will last to the end of time.
Your benefit for beings will be immeasurable.
The benefit of your treasures will last for many
    births throughout many lands.

"After the parinirvana of that life
You will appear in the presence of the victor
    Maitreya.
When Maitreya benefits beings in human form,
You will tame beings as a monk, a Brahmin
    named Palden.

57

> "Again you will benefit beings for seven lives.
> Then all of this will culminate in manifest
> buddhahood."

> This does not come from my knowledge.
> These are the prophecies I received in a vision
> From the great master Padmasambhava.

In response, his two nephews said, "It was extremely kind of you to bestow those prophecies. If, holy one, you are resolved not to remain among us under any circumstances, we pray that you tell us the story of your recollected births."

# Recollection of Previous Births

# Recollection of Previous Births

The guru replied, "My recollections of previous births are too numerous for my tongue to relate. Place in your minds, nephews and others, the brief account that I shall relate based on my dreams and the prophecies I've received.

"The variety of my births is inconceivable. Among the brief and extensive accounts of my recollected previous births, a clear and extensive account of signs of siddhi may be found in the great biography of Saltong Shogom. This is a brief account of Saltong's demonstration of siddhi:

"When the three men from Kham went to India they flew there like birds all the way from Daklha Gampo.[51] They used their shawls as wings and passed through space without impediment. When their guru Gampopa looked at them from where they had started, two of the siddhas appeared to be the size of large birds because of the distance they had flown. Saltong, because of his control of

61

his channels and winds, had flown farther and appeared the size of a small bird.

"When they reached Vajrasana in India they took three relics of Buddha Shakyamuni without impediment, as an exhibition of siddhi.[52] They then collected pills of earth and stone from other sacred places and blessed places, as well as arura berries with their leaves, snake-heart sandalwood, and all other types of medicinal herbs, in order to bring all these things back to Tibet. Then Saltong said to the other two, 'Our guru told the three of us to bring back from the Shitavana charnel ground flesh from a brahmin's corpse, wood from a nyagrodha tree, black stone for carving, earth, stones, and piles of green arura leaves. What are we doing about that?'

"The other two answered, 'The three of us have collected everything that the guru said he needed from Vajrasana. We can't get those things from the Shitavana charnel ground. The flesh-eating dakinis, blood-drinking dakinis, life-stealing dakinis, vitality-robbing dakinis, and breath-collecting dakinis will cast our flesh and blood into the sky! Let us three return to Tibet!'

"Saltong answered, 'Let's not go back yet. We must do what our guru said.'

"The other two said, 'Holy dharma is rarely found in either this or future lives. In order to accomplish holy dharma, you need both a body and a mind. It is certain that at some point body and mind will be separated. Because this human body, with its leisure and resources, is hard to find, we three should return now. We need our bodies!'

"Saltong answered them, 'Doing what your guru says is holy dharma. The guru is the root of holy dharma. Disobedience of your guru's commands is wrongdoing. I am unable to disobey our guru's command!'

"The other two then said, 'In that case, it would be best if you went there.'

"Saltong answered, 'I shall not defy our guru's command. If this body is destroyed by the dakinis, I may obtain a better one through my guru's compassion.'

"After saying that, he flew to the Shitavana charnel ground with the forceful wind of chandali, using his shawl as wings.[53] The other two watched him go, saying as a joke, 'Maybe if he loses that body, through our guru's compassion his next one will have a better-looking face.'

"Saltong flew into the shadow of a mountain shaped like a black snake climbing downward and an elephant lying down. Through the power of his forceful wind of chandali, the dakinis saw him as an inconceivably intense mass of fire. Because his body was of the nature of rainbow light and fire, the dakinis had no way to harm him. From the Shitavana charnel ground he took the flesh of a brahmin's corpse, concealed as treasure; nyagrodha wood; golden victorious arura; the black stone of Shitavana; pills of charnel ground stone; many self-arisen images of dharmapalas in stone; and self-arisen images of the sixteen elders in stone.[54]

"He brought them to Tibet and placed them—the flesh of a seven-birth brahmin, the nyagrodha wood, and the rest—in front of the guru like a feast offering. Then

Saltong sat down and covered his head with his shawl. After three hours the other two arrived. When they saw Saltong sitting there, they said, 'He just went to the Shitavana charnel ground; yet he is already here! We didn't dawdle on the way. We should have got here first. How can this be?' Dismayed, they spoke as if irritated.

"The guru Gampopa said, 'You two worthy siddhas, don't misunderstand. Listen! Saltong Shogom was Tokmay Öden at the time of Vajradhara, Dakpa Sherab at the time of Tilopa, Drogön Lotsa at the time of Naropa, Ngoktön Chöku Dorje at the time of Marpa, and Rechung Dorje Drakpa at the time of Mila. Now, in my time, he is Saltong the Khampa. When the eighty mahasiddhas of India were displaying signs of siddhi, the mahasiddha Tokmay Öden flew through the sky like a bird. He swam through water like a fish. He passed through Mount Meru without impediment. Together with his mudra, he travelled through the sky. Although all the mahasiddhas equally displayed signs of siddhi, only he could pass without impediment through mountains of vajra rock. It was because he was unstoppable in his signs of siddhi that Indians called him Tokmay Öden. Because there was no limit to his siddhi, they also called him Tsemay Öden.[55] That siddha had two names.'

The two other siddhas then asked the guru, "How did he pass without impediment through vajra rock?"

"Gampopa answered, 'When the siddha Tokmay Öden and the siddha Kukuripa were demonstrating signs of siddhi in India, Tokmay Öden, accompanied by his mudra, passed all the way through a nine-peaked mountain of rock. He passed through it downward from its apex to its base, and then upward from its base all the way to its apex. Then he burst out from the mountainside like an arrow. Because his display of such signs of siddhi was unlimited, Indians called him Tsemay Öden. Saltong is his rebirth, and no different than him.'

"The other two then asked, 'Why was he called Öden?'

"The guru Gampopa answered, 'He was called Öden because throughout many births the warm light of his sun will fill the four continents. He will be known by the name "sun." '

"As the other two siddhas were by this time free of doubt, they all—master and disciples—enjoyed a great ganachakra.

"That is a brief account of my demonstration of signs of siddhi. If I were to recount my recollections of previous births extensively, it would be more than my tongue could handle. A brief account is this:

"At the time of the three men from Kham, I was Saltong Shogom. His emanation at the time of Lord Rangjung Dorje was the pandit Ngagi Wangchuk, who was the youngest of three brothers born to a king who guarded the eastern gate of India. Ngagi Wangchuk's story may be found throughout the literature of sutra and tantra.

"His emanation was the realized Trakchuk, whose name became well-known. Displaying the appearance of unpredictability, he tamed all the instantaneously-born gods and spirits through unstoppable miracles and signs of siddhi. In particular, there was a vicious upasaka associated with an iron bridge in Mongolia who could cause the three worlds to shake with his ferocious roar. This upasaka was seen visibly promising obedience to the guru Trakchuk, who thereafter controlled him.[56]

"His emanation was a monk of Shampolung in Tsang named Chökyi Wangchuk. He had many disciples who benefited themselves and others.

"His emanation was born at Karma and held the great seat of Karma Monastery for nine years. He created many excellent supports of body, speech, and mind, and benefited beings immeasurably.

"His emanation was born at Tago in Ga. He served the Buddha's doctrine for thirteen years in order to benefit beings.

"His emanation was born in Lhasa and became known as the monk Sönam Tashi. He turned the dharmachakra greatly for the sangha and achieved immeasurable benefit for beings.

"His emanation was the supreme scholar Sherab Gyamtso, who became renowned for his service to the doctrine.

"His emanation was born at Lek Yakgo, and came to bear the name Kunga Sönam the Birth-Recollector. He became a guru of three regions—Ga, Kyura, and Rong—and benefited beings immeasurably. He was extraordinary. He flew over the Dri River seven times; left seven footprints in stone at Tango in Lo after declaring, 'I am the rebirth of Saltong Shogom;' bound the road-spirit Shatep to samaya; planted his staff into solid rock; caused accomplishment water to appear while he was in Rari;

and demonstrated numerous other wondrous signs of siddhi. He departed for pure realms at Dzonyak.

"His emanation was Tashi Döndrup the Birth-Recollector, whose emanation is me, Nyima Tashi."

The two nephews then said, "It was very kind of you to relate those accounts. Please continue to repeatedly appear as a nirmanakaya!"

The guru Nyima Tashi replied, "I take no delight in rebirth. I would prefer to remain in Sukhavati. Even if I return to Tibet, the whole country will be filled with armies of invasion. An age of sickness, famine, and war will arise. Returning here is bothersome."

The two nephews responded, "Throughout all of greater Tibet—western, central, and eastern—all male and female patrons and all who have entered the gate of dharma have faith in you. For the sake of the future please leave us your skull to serve as a support for prostration, veneration, and circumambulation until you return."

# Relics

# Relics

The guru rubbed his head with his hand and said, "That might happen. Do as much as you can for the benefit of beings and the doctrine. These deities and relics will appear on my skull: between the eyebrows, a white lotus with eight petals will represent the hair that grows there on a buddha. As a sign of my stability in the generation stage, on the right side of my forehead will appear Arya Avalokita. On the left side will appear Machik Lapdrön, surrounded by the mandala of the four families of dakinis. At the fontanel will appear Shakyamuni, our principal teacher. Saraha, the emanation of the victor Vajradhara, will appear holding an arrow as his scepter. In order to guard the realms containing the Buddha's doctrine, the father and mother Realm Protectors will appear. Chökyi Drönma, the emanation of Samantabhadri, will appear with her four sisters and a retinue of dark red carnivorous dakinis.

"Above my left ear will appear Jetsun Milarepa, leaning against a nyagrodha tree and singing his songs. Above my right ear will appear the principal of all mother tantras, Vajravarahi, with her mandala of five deities. At the left of the base of my skull will appear the complete mandala of Shri Chakrasamvara. At the center of the base will appear the wisdom Garuda. As a sign of my mastery of Mahamudra and realization of emptiness, a white AH representing the unborn dharmakaya will protrude from the right side of the base of my skull.

"Mandalas such as those of Vajrasattva, Guhyasamaja, and Hevajra will appear, as will Bernakchen—the mother and the protector inseparable—and the samaya-bound Vajrasadhu. Relic pills the color of fire crystal and water crystal will appear. Among them will be white and red drops and five-colored rainbow light-rays. Within the drops will be innumerable images and relic pills, as colorful and plentiful as masses of clouds. All of these are the deities who will appear on the outside of my skull.

"The deities appearing inside will be these: The principal image will be that of Samantabhadra-Amitabha. Surrounding him will be the buddhas of the five families, the thousand and two buddhas of this fortunate kalpa, the eighty mahasiddhas of India, the eight close sons,[57] the sixteen noble elders, and the victor Vajradhara with the gurus of all lineages—Mahamudra, the path and result, the Great Perfection, five-fold Mahamudra, the middle way, pacification, and the rest—gathered like clouds. The deities of the four tantras and the nine vehicles will appear. The dharmapalas, wealth deities, and all the protectors and guardians of the doctrine of the thousand and two buddhas will appear—powerful, ferocious, and terrifying in appearance—in order to protect the doctrine. Therefore only lamas, spiritual friends, good dharmic people, and patrons whose minds accord with dharma and whose samaya is free of concealment and disruption should see the inside of my skull. It is unfitting for those whose samaya has been disrupted or broken and for wrongdoers with wrong views to see it. If they do, dharmapalas and guardians may resent it and afflict them. Therefore it is not right for the unfit to see it."

The two nephews asked, "If those deities that will appear on your skull were murals, how much space would they occupy?"

The guru replied, "You should say that they would fill a temple with four pillars. Don't say that they would occupy more space than that. If you do, proud, apparent renunciates; malicious, arrogant people; and those tormented by their own bad karma, impure minds, and ignorance might spread the gossip of their wrong views. From now on things are going to get worse and worse. People will become more and more wrong-minded. They will engage in more and more wrongdoing. When divine gurus turn the dharmachakra people will view it as wrong and denigrate it. This will get worse and worse every year. The unfit will say, 'How could so many deities appear in a skull not much bigger than a cup?' It would therefore be best if you were not to say that the deities, if painted, would fill more than a four-pillar temple. In fact, of course, the deities that will appear on my skull could easily fill an eight-pillar temple."

The two nephews then asked, "What is the full extent of these deities? How great is their blessing? What are the benefits of prostration and circumambulation? What is the difference between the compassionate blessing of an artificial image and a self-arisen one? Will those deities all appear at once or gradually? What size will the deities be?"

The guru replied, "If the deities that will appear on my skull were depicted in large murals they could fill a temple with a hundred pillars. The benefit of seeing them is no different from that of pilgrimage to the Vajrasana of Tibet. If fifty-five hundred prostrations accompanied by the generation of bodhichitta or twenty-five hundred circumambulations are performed, these will be equivalent to a hundred million of either. As for their compassionate blessing, one self-arisen image is more wondrous than three artificial ones made of cast metal. The largest deities on my skull will be the size of white mustard seeds. The smallest will be the size of subtle particles. Deities will be perceived even within each of the hairs on my head. As the benefit to beings of this support increases, all the deities will appear."

The nephews then said, "It is very kind of you to tell us of these great wonders. However, if your nirmanakayas do not repeatedly appear, immeasurable benefit for beings will be lost. That would be worse than killing all sentient beings of the three realms!"

Shocked, the guru exclaimed, "How bold! What strong, bold words!"

The two nephews were quite frightened.

Then the guru sang this:

After my parinirvana
Nirmanakayas will appear one after another.
Although it is not my wish to return,
I am concerned about beings' wrongdoing.

I would prefer to stay in Sukhavati
And attend the buddha Amitabha.
It would be delightful to see him
And remain in his presence.
However, I am concerned about beings' wrong-
    doing.

I will therefore benefit beings in Tibet.
Great and continuous nirmanakayas will come.
My name is Nyima Tashi.
In consideration of the benefit my nirmanakayas
    will bring beings,
The name Nyima will not change.

I will leave my skull here.
The hoofprints of my greater and lesser mounts
Are clearly visible at the bottom of Langru.
From now, when I leave you my skull, onward,
Whenever my nirmanakayas pass away,
If they have reached twenty years of age,
Their skulls will remain in one piece of the
    same size.
It would be best to keep them as their principal
    relics.

Emanations of my body, speech, and mind will
    appear.
That will be the sign that the thirty-year life span
    is near.

The arguments and speculation of worldly people
Are like the squawking of parrots.

All my emanations are one without cease
In the expanse of Vajrapani's heart
In the realm of Changlochen.[58]
Therefore I am renowned as Rechung Dorje
    Drakpa.

Sometimes I am renowned as Avalokiteshvara.
Sometimes I am renowned as Vajrapani.
Sometimes I am renowned as Drekpa Kundul.[59]
Sometimes I am renowned as Vajragaruda.

Sometimes I am Drakngak Dongpo.
Sometimes I am Tumpo Zaram.
Sometimes I am the guru Nyenray.
Sometimes I am the great Gushri.
They are all one in the vajra expanse.[60]

In response to that song, one of the disciples inappropri-
ately said to himself, "These are empty words! How could
anyone recollect that many births!" This disciple was very
learned. He possessed unlimited knowledge of liturgical
melodies and other areas of skill. He often praised himself and criticized others, and had no faith in gurus or
spiritual friends. He was arrogant and took a sectarian
and partisan attitude toward other dharma traditions.

The guru immediately knew what the disciple was thinking. Nyima Tashi thought, "This recollection of the three
times in the state of luminous Mahamudra and the Great
Perfection is due to the compassionate blessing of dharma. It has definitely arisen of itself through the power of
samadhi. Nevertheless, beings are running out of good

karma. Buddhas are powerless to prevent that. Beings with terribly bad karma have this problem of wrong views." Thinking that, he gave rise to great compassion for that disciple and continued to think about him. "Yesterday, when I said that proud renunciates and malicious, arrogant people would spread the gossip of wrong views, I thought he might understand. He didn't. Dharma doesn't come easily to sentient beings in these degenerate times! Mara has entered his mind."

Compassionately thinking that, the guru said, "Please gather my two nephews and all the disciples."

When they had all gathered together, the guru admonished them, saying, "What is this talk of proud, vain maras and their wrong views?"

The nephews and all the disciples offered many prostrations accompanied by prayer to their guru and sealed with excellent aspirations. In response, the guru sang this:

> Listen once more, proud nephews!
> This profound account of my lives
> Liberates humans by day and spirits by night.
> If we compare humans and spirits,
> More spirits will be liberated than humans!
>
> This human body is obscured by thick ignorance.
> Human minds are plagued by uncertainty.
> Human mouths babble on.
> Inappropriate doubt and all sorts of wrongdoing
>     arise.
> All the merit accrued throughout all births is
>     used up.
> Hold in your compassion such dharma cynics!

You men and women of precipitous Kham
Would denigrate even the Buddha if he appeared.
Not knowing how to think, you are sectarian
And partisan about philosophical systems.

How can you refute another's outlook
With mere empty attachment and anger?
You incur a downfall and meander in the dark.
No one, laypeople or renunciates, seems to
    know this.

A dark red wind blows out of the All-Doing's
    expanse.
Red tongues of flame swirl out of your mouths.
The ripening of it will be this:
In an instant, you will find yourself in a house of
    fire.
On the outside, it will look like earth and stone.
On the inside, it will be made of black smoke
    and fire.

Like tarnished vases of brass,
You are yellow on the outside and black within,
You arrogant monks!
Will your great arrogance get you through the
    interval?

Because you've never developed an impartial,
    pure outlook,
You've built hell for yourself with your sectarian
    speech.
For sure, if you don't tame your minds,
Loud talk of dharma is a mass of attachment
    and hatred.

The service without concealment
Of great centers for the practice of the Buddha's
    doctrine
And of holy, authentic gurus,
Will increase your merit in this and future lives.

Sycophancy toward leaders brings disaster on
    oneself.
Sycophancy toward relatives invites flesh-debts
    and killers.[61]
Masters and servants waste this life and the next.
To rule a household is to carry the burden of
    others' welfare.

Now, when you have just this once got a human
    body,
It is tragic to waste this life and the next.
Beings in the future, keep this in your minds.
Too much advice just brings derision.

From now on, at all times,
Abandon sectarian attachment and hatred within
    the All-Doing's expanse.
Cultivate impartial, pure outlook within the
    All-Doing's expanse.
Virtue and wrongdoing arise from the All-Doing's
    expanse.
The various philosophical systems that exist
    nowadays,
Whether they are good or bad,
All come from the All-Doing King's expanse.
When virtue arises it is wondrous.
When wrongdoing arises it is depressing.

I have taken many births in Jambudvipa.
I have passed through all four dharma traditions.[62]
I have entered all four of their dharma gates.
I have seen no difference in quality among them,
No reason to say, "This is good and this is bad."

All their dharma leads to buddhahood.
All their dharma comes from the Buddha's mind.
Among all the dharma taught by the Buddha,
He never taught good dharma to one person
And bad dharma to another.
There are no good and bad in the experience of a
    buddha.
Good and bad arise in the experience of
    ignorance.

Throughout many successive births I have helped
    beings
Through Mahamudra, the path and result, five-fold
    Mahamudra,
The dictates as instruction, the Great Perfection,
And each of the dharma traditions and philosophi-
    cal systems.[63]

I therefore have no sectarianism toward philosoph-
    ical systems.
I have been liberated through abandoning sectari-
    an attachment and hatred.
Future followers and disciples, abandon sectarian-
    ism.
Cultivate impartial, pure outlook.
The sources of refuge are infallible.
Keep this in mind.

When the guru had sung that, his nephew Gendun Gyamtso and all those gathered there offered many prostrations. They said to Nyima Tashi, "Guru, thank you very much for your instructions, your accounts of your previous births, your prediction of relics, and your final teachings. May a rain of dharma descend that will establish all sentient beings of the three realms and the four continents, all who live and breathe, both human and nonhuman, in buddhahood. May all be liberated from the great ocean of suffering, samsara, and lower states. May our mothers, all sentient beings throughout space, quickly attain the supreme, unsurpassable state of buddhahood." They made that aspiration.

This completes the account of the births, relics, and final teachings of the Birth-Recollector Nyima Tashi.

> EMA! All authentic gates of profound dharma without exception
> Were taught by this supreme guru. May this pure nectar
> Collected from the lotus grove of his speech
> Cause the benefit of all the doctrine and beings.

This was edited at the behest of the noble lord and embodiment of wisdom and kindness, Drupgyü Tendzin Yeshe Nyima Trinlay Choktu Gyaype De, who said, "As the songs, instructions, recollections of previous births, and description of the relics of this glorious, holy guru are found in so many texts, the sequence and wording of these teachings are uncertain. Please compare these variations to what is found in correct, old texts, and correct the sequence and wording."[64]

When this command was placed on my head, although I lacked the confidence of full understanding, I undertook this task with exertion. I have avoided the impurities of pretty dharma and ornamental words of praise.[65] This was written by one called Suryabhadra, the worst of those disciples cared for by this holy, noble lord throughout all births. I completed it on a good day in the twelfth month of the Earth Dragon Year, my thirtieth year, in the supreme place Palden Tashi Chöling. May it bring spontaneous, great benefit to the doctrine and to beings.

Mangalam bhavantu! Virtue![66]

# A Rain of Blessings

# A Prayer to the Successive Incarnations of the Birth-Recollector Nyima Tashi

The personification of the three jewels' three
    secrets,
Glorious Vajrapani, the Lord of Secrets,
The playful dance of a boundless ocean of
    activity—
I pray to your non-dual embodiment.

The glorious siddha and vidyadhara Tokmay Öden;
His nirmanakaya, Dakpa Sherab;
Drogön Lotsa, the bearer of a treasury of
    compassion—
I pray to the three lords of the ten levels.

Chöku Dorje, the treasury of instructions on
    generation and completion;
Dorje Drakpa, who attained the supreme rainbow
    body;
Saltongpa, who achieved peerless siddhi—

I pray to the three lords among siddhas.

Great pandit Ngagi Wangchuk, beings' protector;
Trakchuk, holder of the treasury of vajrayana;
Dharmeshvara, peerless in the three levels of
    existence—
I pray to the three lords of the doctrine.

Chöwang Palzangpo, who spread the Victor's
    doctrine;
Drogön Trinlay, who held the Buddha's
    teachings;
Sönam Tashi, who possessed the two siddhis—
I pray to the three with empowered activity.

Lord of speech, Sherab Gyamtso;
Protector of beings, Kunga Sönam;
Unfailing single refuge, Tashi Döndrup—
I pray to the three who showed the path to
    liberation.

King of dharma Nyima Tashi [1];[67]
Nyima Gyurmay [2], the emperor's crown jewel;
Supreme Nyima Tenpa Saljay [3], lord of
    siddhas—
I pray to the three peerless sources of refuge.

Chögyal Nyima Wangpo [4], who attained
    supreme bliss-emptiness;
Trinlay Nyima [5], the real Vajrapani;
Great Yeshe Nyima [6], who bestowed the
    supreme appearances of wisdom—
I pray to the three treasuries of compassion.

Exemplary embodiment of the three trainings'
    ornamentation,
Great hidden yogin of perfected siddhi,
Peerless Vajradhara, glory of the doctrine and
    beings—
I pray at the feet of Kunkyap Nyima [7].

Vajrapani, our protector in this degenerate age,
Appearing as a teacher for beings' benefit,
Garland of successive births of the glorious guru—
I pray to you.

Through praying to the noble guru in this way,
May I be cared for by this supreme protector.
May I not be ignorant of the meaning of the scrip-
    tures of Mahamudra,
The path and result, the Great Perfection, the
    middle way, and pacification.
Entering the path of the two stages, may I attain
    manifest and perfect buddhahood.

In all my births may I be of good family and
    intellect, and without pride.
May I be greatly compassionate and devoted to the
    guru.
May I remain within the samaya of the glorious
    guru.

May I never for even a moment give rise to wrong
    views
Of the glorious guru's life.
Through the devotion which sees whatever he does
    as excellent

May the guru's blessing enter my mind.

Throughout all births may I not be separated from
    the authentic guru,
And thus enjoy dharma's splendor.
Having perfected the qualities of the levels
    and paths,
May I quickly attain the state of Vajradhara.

This supplication to the successive incarnations of my
root guru was made with a mind of faith by the one
named Suryabhadra. Shubham.

# Notes

1. The sixth buddha referred to here is the personification of all five sambhogakaya buddha families, not the sixth buddha of this aeon.

2. The name Nyima Tashi means "Fortunate Sun."

3. The three accumulations are moral discipline, merit, and wisdom.

4. Shakyaraja is another name for Buddha Shakyamuni. Throughout this book, wherever the title Buddha is used as a name and refers to the historical buddha, it is capitalized. Otherwise, it is lower case. At this and other points in our text the bodhisattva Vajrapani is described as an emanation of the Buddha's cousin Ananda. In other sources Ananda is often described as an emanation of Vajrapani. In either case, they are said to be different manifestations of a single source of emanation.

5. Sukhavati, "Blissful," is the pure realm of Amitabha.

6. Samaya is the vow binding a disciple to his or her guru and the guru's instructions.

7. Amrita is the legendary elixir of immortality.

8. Kham is the eastern part of the greater Tibetan region.

9. The five poisons are desire, anger, stupidity, pride, and jealousy.

10. Saltong Shogom, "Lucidity-Emptiness, Meditator with a Harelip," was one of Gampopa's three most renowned disciples. As all three were from Kham, they are often called "the three men from Kham." The other two were Düsum Khyenpa, the First Gyalwa Karmapa, and Je Phagmodrupa. Whereas those two were the source of several renowned lineages, Saltong Shogom appears to have had few, if any, human disciples. It is often said that his main activity was to liberate beings in the bardo, the interval between lives, and to teach nonhuman beings. The Traleg Kyabgön Rinpoches, of whom Nyima Tashi was the first, are the recognized rebirths of Saltong Shogom.

11. Dharmakaya, "dharma body," is said to be the true nature of a buddha. It is one of the three bodies of any buddha. The other two are the samboghakaya, "body of complete enjoyment," which is perceived by bodhisattvas; and the nirmanakaya, "body of emanation," which may be perceived by both bodhisattvas and ordinary beings.

12. Pretas are demonic beings afflicted by hunger and thirst. They make up one of the six states of beings. The others are devas or gods, asuras or anti-gods, humans, animals, and hell-beings.

13. The name All-Doing King, Kunjay Gyalpo, is most often found in the Dzokchen or Great Perfection teachings. It is the name of one of the best known tantras of the mind section of the Great Perfection. The All-Doing King is the fundamental mind-in-itself of any sentient being. Although it is pure and perfect in itself, it becomes overwhelmed by the intensity of appearances and fails to recognize them as its own display. This is the source of bewilderment. When the All-Doing King recognizes itself and recognizes appear-

ances to be its own display, it fulfills its inherent potential for manifest perfection. The use of the image of a lamp residing in the chitta or "heart" is a reference to the teachings of the instruction section of the Great Perfection. Nyima Tashi uses the terminology of a variety of meditative traditions in his songs.

14. Mara is the name of the personification of death, and can also refer to beings or mental states that obstruct virtue and liberation. When the term is used as a name, I have capitalized it; when it is used as a more generic term I have not.

15. Yama is the judge of the dead.

16. Shalma Mountain is said to be a hell where the lustful are tormented in the following way. A person born there sees the object of his or her desire at the top of a steep mountain. As the person climbs up the slope, he or she is sliced to ribbons by razor-sharp leaves and thorns. When he or she reaches the top, the object of desire turns into a predatory bird with an iron beak which then pecks out the person's eyes. The person then sees the object of desire at the bottom of the mountain. Climbing down, the person is again sliced to ribbons. Again, when the person reaches the bottom, the object of his or her desire has become a predatory bird with an iron beak, and so on. This can last for thousands of years.

Note that this section of the song is not an isolated criticism of women. Nyima Tashi's point is that even though women in his society lacked the power to do great evil possessed by some men, such as chieftains and their ministers, they were still afflicted by the same obscurations.

17. The six syllables are the mantra of Avalokiteshvara, OM MANI PADME HUM.

18. It is unclear who Gompa Dorje is; Ralpa Kambep is the name of one of Sönam Pel's ancestors.

19. These are the twelve principal deeds of the Buddha: descent from Tushita, birth, mastery of athletics and learning, marriage, renunciation, asceticism, meditation under the tree of

awakening, defeat of Mara, buddhahood, teaching, demonstration of miracles, and parinirvana. Sometimes meditation under the tree of awakening and defeat of Mara are counted as one, in which case either the Buddha's return from the Heaven of the Thirty-Three Devas (where he spent a summer teaching his mother, who had been reborn there) or the posthumous multiplication of his relics is added to the list.

20. The eighteen hells are the eight hot hells, the eight cold hells, the neighboring hells, and the occasional hells.

21. The Monkey month is the sixth month of the Tibetan calendar. The tenth day of that month is associated with Guru Padmasambhava's activity, as is the tenth day of every month. The Glorious Copper-Colored Mountain is the pure realm of Guru Padmasambhava. HRIH is his seed-syllable. Vidyadharas are awakened masters of Vajrayana.

22. According to Khenpo Karthar Rinpoche, this means that false teachers will often loudly proclaim their supposed total disinterest in wealth. They do this in order to so impress others that they are given the very wealth they falsely claim not to seek.

23. Tanglha is an important local divinity and protector of Tibet. Pehar is a protector of monastic wealth and of Tibet in general. Nyens and dralas are powerful nonhumans associated with places, families, and nations. They may be either mundane or supramundane.

24. Manga is Sanskrit for Tashi (Tib.) "auspicious" or "fortunate." This prediction refers to Nyima Tashi.

25. This section of the prophecy refers to a demonic being that seems to be female, although the gender varies in the Tibetan text. She is called Red Kala and Girtika. Red Kala may refer to Kalaratri, the consort of Rudra Bhairava. She is often depicted as red. Girtika is mentioned in a similar prediction in *Chariot of the Fortunate*, a biography of Yongey Mingyur Dorje.

26. Monastics and laity.

27. The three vows are the renunciate's vow of individual liberation, the bodhisattva's vow of bodhichitta, and the vidyadhara's vow of samaya.

28. The Wrathful Guru, here also called "the Guru Heruka," is the name of a number of forms of Guru Padmasambhava seen as a wrathful deity. Tormas are offering cakes. They are sometimes used to avert disaster.

29. This is a prediction of the recovery of a set of instructions concealed by Guru Padmasambhava as treasure. According to Khenpo Karthar Rinpoche, this predicts the recovery of treasure by an incarnation of Traleg Rinpoche. In *Chariot of the Fortunate,* the biography of Yongey Mingyur Dorje, this prediction is cited as referring to his discovery of the Dorje Trolö Cycle. Both Traleg Rinpoche and Yongey Mingyur Dorje Rinpoche are emanations of Vajrapani.

30. The Eight Dispensations are the eight principal yidams of Guru Padmasambhava's tradition. Wisdom Assembly is another cycle taught by Guru Padmasambhava. Its most famous form is Wisdom Assembly of the Guru, a treasure of Sangye Lingpa. Vajrakila is one of the Eight Dispensations, often practiced separately.

31. The deities mentioned here are male and female wrathful deities, all of them buddhas or bodhisattvas depicted in wrathful form. Buddhist wrathful deities are not wrathful in nature, merely in appearance.

32. This is the mantra of Guru Padmasambhava, OM AH HUM VAJRA GURU PADMA SIDDHI HUM.

33. Ushnishavijaya is a female deity associated with protection.

34. Reversal ceremonies employing the mantra OM MANI PADME HUM.

35. Dharanis are spell-like mantras. White Umbrella is a female deity associated with protection.

36. Padampa Sangye was an Indian mahasiddha who brought Vajrayana teachings called "pacification" to Tibet. His greatest disciple was the Tibetan woman Machik Lapdrön, whose teachings are called "severance." Although pacification and severance still exist as separate lineages, severance is held to include the essence of both. In fact, as Guru Padmasambhava says here, severance is regarded as the quintessence of all buddhadharma. The name severance refers to the forceful and abrupt eradication of fixation on a self. One of the principal formats of severance practice is ganachakra or feast practice. The value and benefits of this are described here.

37. The Kabar ceremony is a ritual for the prevention of disaster.

38. The Buddha's teachings can be divided or classified in various ways. One way, based on the circumstances under which a particular teaching was given and its rhetorical style, divides the teachings into twelve branches.

39. Usually the four lineages of severance are enumerated as the father lineage of means, the mother lineage of discernment, the non-dual lineage of the meaning, and the severance lineage of meditation experience.

40. The eighteen emptinesses are eighteen aspects or instances of emptiness.

41. Akanishtha means 'under none'. It can refer to the dharmakaya realm. Here it seems to refer to Sukhavati.

42. The palace of the gods in the Heaven of the Thirty-Three Devas.

43. Matrikas or matriarchs are wrathful female beings. They may be either mundane or supramundane.

44. Surya is "sun" in Sanskrit.

45. Tokmay Öden in Tibetan.

46. Daö Shönnu is the name of one of Gampopa's previous lives. Here, however, it refers to Gampopa himself.

47. Trakchuk literally means "vomiter of blood." He appears to have been a mahasiddha and a disciple of the Third Gyalwang Karmapa, Rangjung Dorje.

48. "The protector of beings" may refer to the Karmapa of the time, most likely the fifth.

49. Nyima means "sun."

50. This is the reason for Khenpo Karthar Rinpoche's statement that the present Ninth Traleg Kyabgön Rinpoche could be the incarnation destined to discover treasure teachings. Guru Rinpoche told Nyima Tashi, the First Traleg Rinpoche, that this incarnation would appear after seven subsequent births, indicating the ninth incarnation.

51. Daklha Gampo was the mountain on which Gampopa's monastery was built. See also note 10.

52. Vajrasana is the site of the Buddha's awakening.

53. Chandali is a yoga of the channels, winds, and drops.

54. The sixteen elders are disciples of the Buddha blessed with extraordinary longevity so that they can continue to guide and protect the Buddha's teachings.

55. Tokmay Öden means "unimpeded light"; Tsemay Öden means "measureless light."

56. An upasaka is a lay disciple. In this case, the lay disciple is non-human and mischievous.

57. The eight close sons are eight bodhisattvas who appeared as disciples of the Buddha.

58. Changlochen is the realm of Vajrapani.

59. Drekpa Kundül, "tamer of all the arrogant," is one of the Eight Dispensations and is considered a form of Vajrapani.

60. Drakngak Dongpo and Tumpo Zaram are emanations of Vajrapani as deities. Nyenray Gendun Bum was a disciple of Karma Pakshi, the Second Karmapa. "The great Gushri," often spelt Goshir in English, seems to refer to His Eminence Gyaltsap Rinpoche, who is an emanation of Vajrapani. Nyima Tashi is proclaiming the single nature of all emanations of Vajrapani.

61. When you kill an animal to eat it or to feed another, you incur what is called a "flesh-debt." Nyima Tashi is saying that this is often the result of trying to please your family.

62. Nyingma, Sakya, Kagyu, and Geluk.

63. Mahamudra, its variation called "five-fold," the path and result, the dictates as instruction, and the Great Perfection are Buddhist traditions still practiced today.

64. According to Khenpo Karthar Rinpoche, Drupgyü Tendzin Yeshe Nyima was a previous Thrangu Rinpoche. The present Thrangu Rinpoche is widely held to be the foremost scholar of the Karma Kagyu tradition. Thrangu Monastery was originally presented to the First Thrangu Rinpoche by the Seventh Karmapa. According to Khenpo Karthar Rinpoche, it was later offered to the Second Traleg Rinpoche by the First Thrangu Rinpoche after the site of Nyima Tashi's practice community was destroyed during a local war.

65. Pretty dharma is spirituality that looks good but is devoid of substance.

66. If the author of this book is the same Suryabhadra who wrote the appended supplication "A Rain of Blessings," the Earth Dragon Year mentioned here is probably 1868, since the supplication stops with the Seventh Traleg Rinpoche, who was alive at that time. According to Khenpo Karthar Rinpoche, the author of both the main account and the appended prayer is a previous Lodrö Nyima Rinpoche. The Lodrö Nyima Tulkus are one of the principal incarnation lines of Thrangu Monastery, along with the Traleg Kyabgön

Rinpoches, the Thrangu Rinpoches, the Zuru Rinpoches, and others. The present Lodrö Nyima Rinpoche is Khenpo Karthar's great nephew.

67. I have inserted numbers after the seven successive Traleg Kyabgön Rinpoches mentioned by name in the prayer.

༄༅། །མཆུངས་མེད་བླ་མ་དམ་པ་ཉི་མ་བཀྲ་ཤིས་ཀྱི་
མགུར་དང་ཞལ་གདམས་སྐྱེ་བ་དྲུན་པའི་རྣམ་ཐར་རྟེན་གྱི་
ལོ་རྒྱུས་བཅས་ཕྱོགས་གཅིག་ཏུ་བཀོད་པ་བཞུགས་སོ།།

༄༅། །མཆུངས་མེད་བླ་མ་དམ་པ་ཉི་མ་བཀྲ་ཤིས་ཀྱི་མགུར་དང་
ཞལ་གདམས་སྐྱེ་བ་དྲན་པའི་རྣམ་ཐར་རྟེན་གྱི་ལོ་རྒྱུས་བཅས་ཕྱོགས་གཅིག་
ཏུ་བཀོད་པ་བཞུགས་སོ།། ན་མོ་གུ་རུ་ རིགས་ཀུན་གཙོ་བོ་དྲུག་པ་རྡོ་རྗེ་
འཆང་། །དབྱེར་མེད་དཔལ་ལྡན་བླ་མ་གཀྲ་བ། །གང་གི་ཕྲིན་ལས་ཉི་མ་
བཀྲ་ཤིས་ཞེས། །ཡོངས་སུ་གྲགས་པ་དེ་ལ་གུས་པས་འདུད། །ཚོགས་
གསུམ་རྒྱ་མཚོའི་དཔལ་ལས་ཤེར་འབྱུངས་པའི། །ཟབ་གསང་རྣམ་པར་
ཐར་པའི་ཕྲེང་བ་ནི། །སྤྲུན་པོའི་དཔལ་ལས་ཕྲ་རབ་རྡུལ་ཕྲན་ཚམ། །ཀུན་
སྟོང་བྱང་ཆུབ་སེམས་ཀྱིས་འདིར་འགོད་བྱ། དེ་ཡང་དཔལ་ལྡན་བླ་མ་
འཇིག་རྟེན་རྣམ་པར་འདྲེན་པ་ཁམས་གསུམ་གྱི་སྐྱབས་གནས་དམ་པ་ཡིད་
བཞིན་ནོར་བུ་རིན་པོ་ཆེ་ལྟ་བུ། སྙིང་བཞི་སྒྲིང་ཕྱན་ཀུན་གྱི་སྨྲག་རྫམ་གསལ་
བའི་སྒྲོན་མེ་རྗེ་འགྲན་གྱི་བླ་མེད་ཉི་མ་བཀྲ་ཤིས་དེ་ཉིད་སྟོང་པ་ཉིད་ཀྱི་དོན་

101

ཏོགས། ཕྱུག་རྒྱུ་ཆེན་པོ་ལ་མངའ་བརྙེས། མཚམས་འདེགས་སྤྱིར་ལ་ཅེ་
གཅིག་ཏུ་དགུང་ལོ་མང་པོར་བཞུགས་པའི་སྐབས་སུ་རྩ་ལྷས་དང་ཕྲུང་ལྷས་
མཛད་པས་རྩ་ཕྲུང་ཐིག་གསུམ་ལ་རང་དབང་ཐོབ་པའི་རྟགས་སུ་སྨྲེ་བ་བརྒྱ་
དང་བརྒྱད་ཅུ་ཟུན་པས་སྨྲེ་དྲུན་བརྒྱ་བརྒྱད་ཅུ་ཞེས་ཡོངས་སུ་གྲགས་སོ། །
དེ་ནས་སྨྲེ་བ་མང་པོའི་གོང་རོལ་དུ་ཤུ་གུའི་རྒྱལ་པོ་ཐུབ་པ་ཆེན་པོའི་དུས་ན་
གུན་དགའ་པོ་དེ་ཉིད་ཀྱིས་སྤྱལ་པ་མཐའ་ཡས་པར་བསྐོན་པ་ལས། ཕྱུག་
ན་རྡོ་རྗེའི་རིགས་ལ་སྤྱལ་པ་བསམ་གྱིས་མི་ཁྱབ་པར་སྤྱལ་ནས་རྟ་འཕུལ་
བསྐན་པའི་དུས་སུ་རང་ཕྱུག་ན་རྡོ་རྗེ་ཨུ་ཙ་ཡ་དག་སྤྱགས་ཀྱི་སྲོང་པོ་ཞེས་
བྱ་བའོ། །སྨྲེ་བ་གོང་རོལ་དེའི་ཕྱིན་ཆད་དང་ད་ལྟ་ཡན་གྱི་སྨྲེ་བ་དྲུན་པའི་ལོ་
རྒྱུས་དང་། འགྲོ་དོན་མཛད་པའི་རྣམ་ཐར་དང་ཕྱུགས་རྗེ་ཆེ་བའི་དགར་ཆག་
བསམ་གྱིས་མི་ཁྱབ་པའི་སྒྲེ་གས་བམ་པོ་དི་དོ་མཚར་བའི་ཆེད་དུ་རྒྱས་པར་
བཀོད་པ་དང་། ཡང་ཐེབ་མ་གསུམ་ཅུ་ཡར་ཐོག་གཅིག་གཏན་ལ་ཕབ་ཀྱང་ཉེ
གནས་དན་པ་ཞིག་གིས་རྗེན་འབྲེལ་མ་འཆམས་པའི་གཏམ་འདི་ལྟར།
ཁྱེད་ཀྱི་སྐུ་ཆེ་བའི་ཡོན་ཏན་དེ་ཚམ་ཞིག་དབུ་ནག་པའི་རིང་ལ་མཛད་མི་
འདུག་པས། ད་དབུ་དཀར་བའི་རིང་ལ་ཅེ་བྱ་ཞུས་པས། པོ་ཁྱེད་བདེན་ནོ་
གསུངས་ནས་མདུན་མེ་ཡོད་པའི་ནང་དུ་རྣམ་ཐར་བྲིས་ཤིན་པ་རྣམས་
བསྲེགས༔ དེ་ཡང་ཉེ་གནས་དེ་ཡིས་རྗེན་འབྲེལ་མ་འཆམས་པར་སྨྲས་པ་
ལས་བྱུང་། དེ་ནས་བླ་མའི་ཕྱགས་དགོངས་མཛད་པས་རང་ཉིད་ཀྱི་སྐུ་ལུས་
ཀྱང་མི་རྟག་པས་འཇིག་རན་པར་མཁྱེན་ནས། ང་ཉིད་མི་འདུག་བདེ་བ་
ཅན་དུ་འགྲོ་རན་གསུངས་ནས་མི་རྟག་པའི་མགྱུར་མ་འདི་གསུངས་སོ། རྗེ

༄༅། །རྒྱ་བའི་བླ་མ་རིན་པོ་ཆེ། །ངེས་འབྱུང་སྙིང་ནས་སྐྱེ་བར་བྱིན་གྱིས་རློབས། །འདུས་བྱས་འཁོར་བའི་ཆོས་ལ་སྙིང་པོ་མེད། །མི་རྟག་མི་རྟག་སྙིང་པོ་མེད། །འགྱུར་ཞིང་འགྱུར་ཞིང་སྙིང་པོ་མེད། །གཡོ་ཞིང་གཡོ་ཞིང་སྙིང་པོ་མེད། །འཇིག་ཅིང་འཇིག་ཅིང་སྙིང་པོ་མེད། །ངང་རང་ལོ་རྒྱུས་སྙིང་པོ་མེད། །འཁོར་བའི་ཆོས་ལ་སྙིང་པོ་མེད། །ཕྱི་སྣོད་ཀྱི་འཇིག་རྟེན་ཡང་གཡོ་ཞིང་འཇིག །ནང་བཅུད་ཀྱི་སེམས་ཅན་ཡང་གཡོ་ཞིང་འཇིག །མཐོ་རིས་བླ་སྐར་གསུམ་ཡང་གཡོ་ཞིང་འཇིག །དམའ་ས་གནའི་རི་བྲག་ཀྱང་གཡོ་ཞིང་འཇིག །བར་སྣང་གི་ལྷོ་སྤྲིན་ཡང་གཡོ་ཞིང་འཇིག །ཕྱུ་ཏུ་བོའི་གནས་དཀར་ཡང་གཡོ་ཞིང་འཇིག །མདའ་གཅང་ཆབ་སྟོན་མོ་ཡང་གཡོ་ཞིང་འཇིག །གཡས་རི་བྲག་དང་རྗེ་ཤིང་ཡང་གཡོ་ཞིང་འཇིག །གཡོན་རི་སྦྱང་ལྱང་དང་མེ་ཏོག་ཀྱང་གཡོ་ཞིང་འཇིག །དུས་དབྱར་དགུན་སྟོན་དཔྱིད་ཀྱང་གཡོ་ཞིང་འཇིག །ཞམ་ཆེན་མཆན་ལོ་བླ་ཡང་གཡོ་ཞིང་འཇིག །ཆུལ་དེ་སོགས་གཡོ་བའི་རྣམ་འགྱུར་ཡིན། །ཡང་འོ་སྐོལ་འཇིག་རྟེན་སྐྱེ་འགྲོ་རྣམས༔ །སྒྱིང་བཞི་གྱིང་ཕུན་བསྐོར་ཀྱང་སྙིང་པོ་མེད། །ལོངས་སྤྱོད་མངའ་ཐང་རྒྱས་ཀྱང་སྙིང་པོ་མེད། །གོ་མཚོན་བུ་ཏུ་འཛོམ་ཡང་སྙིང་པོ་མེད། །ཕ་མ་ཉེ་འབྲེལ་འཛོམ་ཡང་སྙིང་པོ་མེད། །བདེ་སྐྱིད་སྣན་གྲགས་ཆེ་ཡང་སྙིང་པོ་མེད༔ །བཙན་ཕྱུག་དར་གསུམ་འཛོམ་ཡང་སྙིང་པོ་མེད། །མཐོ་བླ་མའི་གདན་ས་ཡང་གཡོ་ཞིང་འཇིག །འོག་དགེ་འདུན་གྱི་འདུ་ར་ཡང་གཡོ་ཞིང་འཇིག །སྟོབས་རྒྱལ་སྲིད་ཀྱི་འབྱོར་པ་ཡང་གཡོ་ཞིང་འཇིག །བྲོ་དགའ་གཉེན་གྱི་རྟག་འཛོན་ཡང་གཡོ་ཞིང་འཇིག །བར་ཐམས་ཅད་མི་རྟག་གཡོ་

ཞིང་འརིག །སྐྱེ་བ་འདི་དབྱར་གྱི་རྩེ་ཐོག་དང་འདྲ། །ཆུས་པ་འདི་མགུལ་
རྒྱན་པོ་རྡོ་དང་འདྲ། །ཁ་བ་འདི་བྱེ་ཚོན་གྱི་ཉ་དང་འདྲ། །འཆི་བ་འདི་ཉི་
ཟེར་གྱི་བ་མོ་དང་འདྲ། །གཉེན་འདུན་འདི་ཉལ་སའི་ཚོར་མ་དང་འདྲ། །
ནོར་རྫས་འདི་འཛད་ཚོན་གྱི་རི་མོ་དང་འདྲ། །ཕྱི་མ་འདི་ས་བོན་གྱི་ལོ་ཐོག
དང་འདྲ། །སྣང་བ་འདི་རྨ་མའི་ཚོང་འདུས་དང་འདྲ། །རང་སེམས་འདི་
གཡའ་དག་གི་ནམ་མཁའ་དང་འདྲ། །སྐྱིར་འདུས་བྱས་ལ་སྙིང་པོ་མ་མཆིས་
ཤིང་། །སྐྲོས་འགྱོ་བའི་ཚེ་སྲོག་ལ་རྟག་འཛིན་མེད། །དོན་མེད་ཀྱི་ལས་ལ་
མ་ཡེངས་པར། །དོན་ལྡན་གྱི་དགར་པོའི་དགེ་བ་སྐྲུབས། །ཞེས་གསུངས་
ཏེ། །བོད་ལ་དབོན་པོ་སྐྲུ་མཆེད་གཉིས་ཀྱིས་ཞུས་པ། དེ་མ་གསུངས་ད་ལོ་
ཚམ་བཞགས་པར་ཞུ་ཞེས་ཞུས་པ་ལ། བླ་མས་དེ་མ་གནང་ནས་འདི་སྐྱུང་
ཅེས་གསུངས་སོ། །། བརྒྱུད་ལྡུན་བླ་མ་རིན་པོ་ཆེ། །མི་འབྲལ་སྤྱི
བོའི་རྒྱན་དུ་བཞུགས། །གསོལ་བ་འདེབས་སོ་ཧིང་ང་རང་འགྲོ། །མ་ཉམ་
པར་བཞག་ཅིང་། །ཐབ་ལམ་བསྒོམ་ཞིང་། །དག་ཚིག་བསྒྲུང་ཞིང་། །དག
སྐྱང་སྐྱོངས་ཤིང་། །སྐྱང་བ་ལམ་དུ་འབྱེར་ཞིང་། །གནས་ལ་ཆགས་ཞེན་
མེད་ཅིང་། །གཉེན་ལ་གདུང་སེམས་མེད་ཅིང་། །གྲོགས་ལ་སྐྱོ་ཤས་མེད་
བཞིན། །ཟས་ལ་སྲེད་པ་མེད་བཞིན། །ཉོར་ལ་ཆགས་ཞེན་མེད་བཞིན། །
སྐྱིང་ནས་བླ་མ་བསྒོམ་ཞིང་། །འཕོ་བ་འདའ་ལྱར་འཕེན་ཅིང་། །ཕ་བླ་མའི་
ཐུགས་ཀར་འཕོ་བར་བྱ། །ཞེས་གསུངས་པས། ད་ཅིས་ཀྱང་མི་བཞུགས
འཕྲིན་ན་འང་། དེད་འདིར་འཚོགས་རྣམས་ལ་ཚོས་ཐུན་ཞལ་གདམས་རེ
གསུངས་པར་ཞུ་ཞེས་ཞུས་པས། བླ་མའི་ཞལ་ནས། ། རྗེ་དུས་གསུམ་

༄༅། །སངས་རྒྱས་འགྲོ་བའི་མགོན། །མགོན་གཅིག་བསྲུས་དཔལ་
ལྡན་བླ་མ་མཆོག །མཆོག་གསུམ་གྱི་ངོ་བོ་དྲིན་ཅན་རྗེ། །རྗེ་བླ་མས་སྐྱོང་
བར་མཛད་དུ་གསོལ། །གནས་བདེ་བའི་འདུ་བའི་ཁང་ཁྱིམ་ཡང་། །རང་
ཕར་ཕར་འགྲོ་དུས་སྐྱར་ནས་འཛོག །འཕལ་བྱམས་བྱམས་འདུ་བའི་ཉེ་དུ་
ཡང་ྋ །དབུགས་ཐུད་ཐུད་ཆད་དུས་དུ་ཞིང་གདུང་། །འཕལ་སྣེན་སྣེན་
གདམ་གྱིས་མགོ་བསྐོར་ཡང་། །འདི་ཕན་ཕན་མི་འོང་གནོད་པའི་རྒྱུ། །
ལུས་མཛེས་མཛེས་ཆགས་པའི་གྲུན་སྐྱོང་འདེས། །རྒྱུན་བཟང་བཟང་དག
གིས་སྣས་གྱུར་ཀྱང་། །སྒོག་དང་དང་རྒྱུབ་འགག་དུས་སྲ། །གཉེན་བྱམས་
བྱམས་རྗེ་སྤྱར་མད་ན་ཡང་། །བདུད་འཛིགས་འཛིགས་འཚེ་བདག་གིས་
ཟིན་ཚེ། །མིག་ཐིག་ཐིག་གདོང་ལ་ལྟ་བྱེད་ཅིང་། །ཡུས་འགྲི་འགྲི་སྟེ་
སྐྱགས་འདོན་པ་ཚམ། །དུས་འཕལ་འཕལ་དམ་ཆོས་མ་བསྒྲུབ་ན། །
སེམས་གཡེང་གཡེང་དང་དུ་མི་ཚེ་ཟད། །དུས་ཡང་ཡང་འཁོར་བའི་སྐྱབས
སུ་ཆུད། །དེ་ཡང་ཡང་ཆུད་ཅིང་ཡང་ཡང་འཁོར། །ད་དགའ་དགའ་འདུ་
ཡང་དགེ་སྦྱོར་འབུངས། །འཕལ་སྲོག་སྲོག་འདུ་ཡང་དགའ་སྤྱུད་ཀྱིས། །
ལག་བདེ་བདེ་འདུ་ཡང་མི་དགེ་སྦྱོངས། །གནས་སྙིང་སྙིང་འདུ་ཡང་འཁོར་
བ་སྦྱོངས། །སྣ་དགར་དགར་ལོ་ནས་མགོ་པོ་གཡོགས། །གཟུགས་
ལོག་ལོག་གཉེར་མས་ལུས་ཀུན་ཁྱབ། །ལུས་སྐྱར་སྐྱར་འཕར་བ་ལ་བརྟེན
ཅིང་ྋ །སེམས་ཞུམ་ཞུམ་བྱ་བ་བྱེད་མི་ནུས། །འཕལ་དགའ་དགའ་འདུ་
བའི་དངོས་པོ་རྣམས། །གཞན་དགའ་དགའ་ཞིག་གིས་སྤྱོད་རྒྱ་ལས། །
རང་ཐམ་ཐམ་གཅིག་ཕྱར་འགྲོ་དུས་སྲ། །ཞོར་ཆུང་ཆུང་ཚམ་ཡང་ཁྱེར

དབང་མེད། །ད་དུང་དུང་འཆི་བ་སྟིང་ནས་སོམས། །ཕན་ཚེས་ཚེས་དམ་
པའི་ལྷ་ཆོས་སྒྲུབས། །སྐྱད་ལྤང་ལྤང་བྲ་མར་གསོལ་བ་ཐོབ། །ཡིད་དུང་
དུང་མོས་གུས་ཁོ་ནར་སྒྲིལ། །འཕྲལ་ལེགས་ལེགས་ཆེ་འདིའི་འདུན་མ་
ཐོངས། །ཁྲི་གསལ་གསལ་འདུ་བའི་སྐྱང་བ་འདི། །ཚོན་ཡོད་ཡོད་སྐྱང་
ཡང་སྐྱི་ལམ་འདུ། །སྐྱ་ཁྲོལ་ཁྲོལ་སྐྱུ་ཚོགས་གྲགས་པ་འདི། །སྟོང་ལྤང་
ལྤང་བྲག་ཅ་གྲགས་དང་མཚུངས། །སེམས་རིག་རིག་སྐྱུ་ཚོགས་འཆར་བ་
འདི། །གང་ཕར་ཕར་བྲོ་འདས་རིག་པའི་རྩལ། །སེམས་རང་རང་ངོ་བོ་
བཙལ་ན་ལེགས། །འཕྲལ་བདེན་བདེན་འདུ་བའི་ཚོགས་བཅད་འདི། །
བློར་ལྷལ་ལྷལ་ཕར་ནས་སྨྲས་པ་ཡིན། །འདི་འདུ་འདུ་འདུག་ན་གཞིན།
འཕྲེལ་མཛོད། །ཚིག་སྐྱན་སྐྱན་འདུག་ན་ཞར་ལ་ཐོན། །ཡར་མིན་མིན་
འདུན་རྒྱུབ་ཏུ་སྐྱུར། །ཚིག་འགྱིག་འགྱིག་འདུ་བའི་ཅ་ཅའི་གཏམ། །ཏོན་
ཆེ་ཆེ་ཡོད་པ་མ་མཐོང་ཡང་། །དེ་ཡང་ཡང་ནེ་ཚོས་སྐྲུས་བཞིན་ནོ། །ཞེས་
རྦུང་ལྷུན་གྱི་ཚིགས་བཅད་འདི་ཡང་ཁྱུང་རྗོང་དུ་སྐྲུས་པའོ།། ཡང་འདི་སྐང་
ཅེས་གསུངས། ༈ ཀྱེ་ཧོཿ མ་ཡེ་ངས་གསོན་དང་སྐྱལ་ལྤན་འདིར་
འདུས་རྣམས། །གཅུང་རོང་འཁོར་བའི་རྒྱ་མཚོ་ཆེན་པོ་ལས། །ཐར་དང་
མི་ཐར་རང་གི་ལས་ལ་རག །ལུས་ངན་འཁོར་བའི་ས་ཁྲག་འདམ་རྫབ་
འདི། །དམ་ཚོས་སྒྲུབ་པའི་སྟོད་དང་ལྷན་ན་མཆོག །ཕྱིག་པའི་སྟོད་ནས་
གྱུར་ན་འཁོར་བར་འཁྱམས། །བླ་མའི་གདམས་ངག་བདུང་རྗེ་ལྷ་བུ་འདི། །
ནད་ཐོག་སྐྱན་བཞག་བཞིན་དུ་ཉམས་སུ་ལོངས། །ལོག་པར་ལྟ་བའི་དུག
ངན་མ་འཐུང་ཞིག །ད་རེས་ལུས་འདི་སྟོང་ཟད་མ་ཕོར་ཅི། །སྟོང་ཟད

༄༅། །སོང་ན་གོང་ཚབ་ཆེན་པོ་ཡིན། །འཛམ་གླིང་ར་བ་རོར་གྱིས་གང་བ་ལས། །བླ་མའི་གདམས་ངག་ཉིན་གཅིག་སྒྲུབ་པ་མཆོག །འཛམ་གླིང་རབ་བང་མཛོད་གྱུར་པ་ལས། །བླ་མའི་ཞབས་འབྲིང་ཉིན་གཅིག་སྒྲུབ་པ་མཆོག །འཇིག་རྟེན་ཟས་ནོར་འཛམ་གླིང་གང་བ་བས། །ལུས་ངག་དགེ་སྦྱོར་ཉིན་གཅིག་འབད་པ་མཆོག །མཆོག་ཏུ་གྱུར་པ་དཀར་པོའི་དགེ་བ་སྒྲུབས༔ །དུག་བཞིན་འཛེམ་པ་ནག་པོའི་སྡིག་པ་སྤོངས། །རང་གི་ལུས་ལ་དཔེའི་ལོངས་དང་ནི། །མདའ་མདུང་རལ་གྱི་ལ་སོགས་མི་དགོས་ཏེ༔ །རང་ལུས་འདི་ལ་ཁབ་གཅིག་ཆུགས་དང་ནི། །ཞ་ཚེ་ཆེ་ཆུང་རང་གི་ལུས་ལ་སྐྱེས། །ཕ་རོལ་སེམས་ཅན་ལུས་ལ་འབང་ངེ་དང་མཆུངས། །དེ་འདྲ་ལུ་བཀྲ་རང་གི་ལུས་ལ་སྐྱོང་། །ན་ཚའི་སྡུག་བསྔལ་དེ་བས་དགུ་འགྱུར་ཆེ༔ །དེས་ན་རང་ལུས་འདི་ལ་དཔེ་ལོངས་ཤིག །དེ་བཞིན་སེམས་ཅན་ཀུན་གྱི་ལུས་ལ་ནི། །གནོད་པ་མ་བསྐྱལ་རང་ཉིད་ཁོ་ནར་སྐྱིན། །གཙང་རོང་ཁམས་ཀྱི་མི་ནག་པོ་མོ་རྣམས། །ཡིད་ལ་ཞིག་དང་སྙིང་གི་བླ་བོ་ཡིན། །སྤྱིད་པའི་གྲུ་དབུངས་ཙོ་གའི་སྣང་འགྱུར་འད། །བརྟོད་པ་དོན་མེད་ཡིན་ནོ། །ཡིད་ལ་ཞིག །སེར་སྣམས་བསགས་པའི་ནོར་རྫས་གང་ཡོད་རྣམས། །ཕྱི་མའི་ལམ་གྱི་གྲོ་ཕྱེ་མ་ཐུབ་ན། །འདི་ནི་སྟོང་གསོག་ཡིན་པ་ཡིན་ལ་ཞིག །ལོ་བརྒྱ་ལོན་ཀྱང་དམ་ཆོས་མ་བསྒྲུབ་ན། །ཉིན་མོ་ལྷ་བཅུར་རྣམ་གཡེང་འཁྲུལ་པའི་ལས། །མཚན་མོ་ལྷ་བཅུར་གཏི་མུག་རོ་ཉལ་སོང་། །ལོ་བརྒྱ་ལོན་པ་དེ་ན་སྟོང་ཟད་ཤོར། །དེ་བས་མི་ཚང་མནའ་སྙིག་ཅུབ་ཐོབ་བྱེད། །གཙང་རོང་ཁམས་ཀྱི་ལས་དན་ཕྱུགས་རྗེས་ཟུངས། །འི་སྐྱོལ་སེར་གོས་ཀྱིན

107

པའི་མེར་མོ་རྣམས། །འགགར་མིན་ཡིན་མདོག་དག་དག་རྡོག་རྡོག་བྱེད། །
སྟོང་སྐྱད་མཐོན་པོས་ཀྱིར་དབུངས་རེལ་བུ་འཕྲོལ། །མི་ཡིས་བསགས་པའི་
ནོར་རྫས་སྟུ་དག་ལེན། །རང་གི་ཚོས་རྒྱགས་ལྷ་འཕྲི་རྟེན་བཞིངས་
སོགས། །དད་པས་མཆོད་པ་སྟྲིན་པའི་ཞིང་ས་ལ། །རན་རྡོག་ཙམ་ཞིག་
མཆོད་སྟྲིན་མ་བྱ་བས། །ཞི་ལོག་དམ་བསྒྱུར་མནའ་སྲོག་དགུ་འགྱུར་
འགྲོ། །དགོར་གྱི་ཞི་བསྐྱེད་དུག་གི་སྟོང་པོ་འདུ། །ཞི་བསྐྱེད་བྱས་ཀྱུ་ཚོས་
ཙར་སོང་བ་ན། །མཆོག་ཏུ་གྱུར་པ་དགོར་གྱི་གསོག་འཛོག་ཡིན། །མི་ཙ་
ཡིན་ཟེར་མི་ནག་པོ་མོ་ལ། །དགོར་གྱི་གསོག་འཛོག་དེ་ཡི་ལག་ཏུ་
བླུགས། །དུག་གི་སྟོང་པོ་ཡུངས་གཞི་མར་ལོག་ཡིན། །དེ་འདྲ་མ་བྱེད་
བསགས་པ་ལམ་ལོག་གོ །རང་གི་ཁ་རྒྱབ་གཉིས་པོ་བྱས་པའི་རྗེས། །
ལྷག་མ་ཅི་འདུག་དགོན་མཆོག་ཕྱོགས་སུ་ཕོངས། །བདག་གཞན་གཉིས་
ཡོད་ཡིན་པས་ཡིད་ལ་ཞོག །དིང་སང་ཚོས་པ་ཡིན་ཟེར་སྨྲ་པོ་ཆེ། །རང་གི་
ཤེས་རྒྱུད་མ་དུལ་ཉིང་རེ་བ། །ཤེས་རྒྱུད་གོག་པོ་འདི་ལ་ཨན་ཅིག་ཕོབ། །
རང་གི་ཁ་ལག་འཕྲེལ་བའི་ཤི་གསོན་ལ། །བྱམས་དང་སྟིང་རྗེ་ཆེན་པོ་རྒྱུན་
དུ་སྐོམས། །རང་ཆེ་དུག་ལྷུའི་རྣང་ནག་འཁྲུབ་མ་འདི། །བྱམས་དང་སྟིང་
རྗེའི་ཞགས་པས་རྒྱུན་དུ་ཆིངས། །ཞི་སྡང་དམར་ནག་མེ་རི་འབར་བའི་
ཚོབས། །སྟོང་ཉིད་སྟིང་རྗེའི་ཆུ་རྒྱུན་ཕབ་པས་ཐུལ། །དི་རྣམས་རང་
སེམས་གསལ་བའི་ཀྱོང་དུ་ཞོག །སེམས་ལ་ཞིག་དང་སྟིང་གི་བྱ་པོ་ཡིན། །
ཞེས་ཞལ་ཆེམས་འདི་རྣམས་སེར་མོ་བ་དང་འགྲོ་བ་སྟྱི་ལ་གསུངས་པ་དང་།
དེ་ནས་དཔོན་སློན་རྣམས་དང་། གཙོ་བོ་རྣམས་དང་། ཕ་ཁུ་རྣམས་དང་།

108

༄༅། །བུ་གཞོན་རྣམས་དང་། མ་སྲུ་ཏུས་པ་རྣམས་དང་། གཞོན་ནུ་མ་རྣམས་ལ་རིག་གྱིས་འདི་ཕྱི་གཉིས་གཅིག་ཏུ་དྲིལ་བའི་ཚོས་ཐུན་ཞལ་ཆེམས་སུ་སྤྲལ་བ་ནི། ༈ ཨེ་མ་ཧོཿ ཕྱག་ཆེན་ལྷ་བའི་ནམ་མཁའ་ཡངས་པ་ལ། །རྟོགས་པ་ཆེན་པོ་ནམ་མཁའི་འཇའ་དང་དང་འདྲ། །སེམས་ཉིད་འོད་གསལ་འཁོར་འདས་ཀུན་ཁྱབ་འདི། །རྒྱུ་རྐྱེན་མ་ནུབ་གསལ་སྟིབ་མེད་པ་འདྲ། །བཀའ་བརྒྱུད་རིན་པོ་ཆེ་ལ་ཕྱག་འཚལ་བསྟོད། །གསལ་སྟོང་སྒོམ་པོའི་སྐྱེ་བ་བརྒྱུད་པ་ཡི། །རིག་པའི་མཐའ་རྒྱུར་ཉི་མ་བཀྲ་གིས་ངས། །ཁྱེད་རྣམས་སེམས་ལ་བཟང་ངན་གང་ཤར་དེ། །ང་ཡི་སྟོང་བ་ཚོས་སྐུའི་དང་ལ་གསལ། །ཕི་ཚོག་སེམས་ལ་མ་ཕོར་སྐྱལ་ལྡན་ཉིན། །དུས་ངན་སྙིགས་མར་སེར་སྐྱུ་དུག་ཞེན་མེད། །རྒྱལ་ཁམས་ཡོངས་ཀྱི་མི་ནག་པོ་མོ་ཡི། །རང་ཚོད་མི་ཤིན་ཏུ་བྱེད་དགུང་ལ་སྐུར། །དེ་འདྲ་མ་བྱེད་བུ་སྟོང་ལས་ལོག་ཡིན། །འི་སྐྱོལ་འདིར་འཚོགས་གས་པོ་མོ་ཐམས་ཅད་ནི། །པོ་ནི་གཅིག་སོང་གཉིས་སོང་འཆི་ལ་ཉེ། །ཟླ་བ་གཅིག་སོང་གཉིས་སོང་འཆི་ལ་ཉེ༔ །ཞག་པོ་གཅིག་སོང་གཉིས་སོང་འཆི་ལ་ཉེ། །གཅུང་རོང་འཁོར་བའི་མི་ནག་པོ་མོ་རྣམས། །དགེ་དང་མི་དགེ་མང་པོ་བསྐྱལ་ལོང་མེད། །མང་པོ་བསྐྱབས་ཀྱང་རང་མགོ་འཁོར་བའི་རྒྱུ། །མང་པོ་མ་སྐྱབས་བསམ་པ་ཚོས་ལ་ཕོངས། །འདི་ཕྱི་གཉིས་ཡོང་ཡིན་པས་ཡིན་ལ་ཞོག །འདི་ནས་པ་རོལ་འགྲོ་བའི་ལམ་སོ་ལ། །ཁྲིམ་གྱི་བཟའ་ཚང་གང་ཡོད་ཐམས་ཅད་ནི། །ཕན་པ་ཅུང་ཟད་མེད་ཅིང་གཏོད་པའི་རྒྱུ། །མིག་ནས་ཁྲག་གི་མཆི་མའི་དུག་ཆར། །འབབ༔ །འོ་དོད་མང་པོ་བོས་པས་གཡང་སར་ལྱུང་། །ཕྱི་རབས་གཞོན་

པོ་འདི་ན་ལུས་པ་ཚོ། །གཤིན་པོ་ཚེ་འདས་སྐྱོན་དུ་སོང་བ་ལ། །འི་དོད་
མཆེ་མའི་དུག་ཆར་མ་འབེབས་ཤིག །སྲི་འགྲོ་སེམས་ཅན་མཐོ་དམན་
ཐམས་ཅད་ནི། །གདོས་བཅས་ལུས་འདི་མི་རྟག་པོར་བའི་དུས། །འི་དོད་
ཆེན་པོས་ཐན་པ་ག་ལ་ཡོད། །འི་དོད་ཆེན་པོའི་རྒྱ་དྲང་དུ་འབོད་འདིས། །
གཤིན་པོ་དེ་དག་ཞེ་ཁགས་སེམས་ཡུལ་འཁྲུལ། །དྲང་སྲུང་ཆེན་པོས་ཐན་
མེད་དམྱལ་བ་ལ། །སྐྱང་ཉེན་ཡོང་བས་འི་དོད་མ་འབོད་ཅིག །འགྲོ་བ་མི་
ནག་པོ་མོ་ལ་སོགས་པའི། །མཐོ་དམན་ཀུན་གྱི་ཡིད་ལ་དེ་ལྟར་ཞིག །སྲིད་
གསུམ་མི་རྟག་བར་སྣང་སྒྱིན་དང་འདྲ། །འདུ་འཛམ་མི་འདུ་དབྱར་དགུན་དུས།
བཞི་ལ། །མི་རྟག་སྐྱུ་འགྱུར་སྟོ་འགྱུར་དབྱར་དགུན་འགྱུར། །དབྱར་ཟླ་
གསུམ་དང་སྟོན་ཟླ་གསུམ་པོ་ལ། །ས་ཡི་དོད་ཀྱིས་གྲང་བའི་སེར་བུ་
འཛོམས༔ །ཆེ་ཤིང་ནགས་ཆལ་མེ་ཏོག་ཤིན་ཏུ་བཀྲག །དགུན་ཟླ་གསུམ་
དང་དཔྱིད་ཟླ་གསུམ་པོ་ལ། །ས་ཡི་དོད་ཡལ་ཆེ་ཤིང་ནགས་ཆལ་རྣམས། །
དེ་ཡང་མི་རྟག་འགྱུར་བས་འབྱུང་བ་འཛིག །ནམ་ཟླ་དུས་བཞིའི་འགྱུར་
ལུགས་འདི་ལ་སྟོས། །འི་སྐྱོལ་ལུས་འདི་དག་ཀྱང་མི་རྟག་ན། །མི་རྟག་པ་
ལ་རྟག་པར་མ་འཛིན་ཅིག །འི་སྐྱོལ་འདིར་ཚོགས་མཐོ་དམན་ཐམས་ཅད་
ཀྱིས༔ །དལ་འབྱོར་མི་ཡི་ལུས་འདི་རྙེད་ཐོག་འདིར། །སྟོང་ལོག་མ་ཤོར་
ཚམ་ཞིག་མ་ཐུབ་ན། །འདི་ནས་ཕ་རོལ་འགྲོ་བའི་ལམ་སོ་ན། །དགྱལ་
བའི་བསུ་མ་སྟོན་སྣུག་ཡོད་རབ་འདུག །དགི་ཤིག་འཕྲས་བུ་སོ་སོར་སྣིན་
རབ་འདུག །སྟོན་ནངས་རྒྱས་མང་པོའི་ཨ་གུ་ཡིན་སྐད་ལ། །དཔེ་རྒྱུང་
མང་པོའི་ཡིན་མིན་པོས་སྣད་ལས། །དགི་ཤིག་སོ་སོའི་ཤན་འབྱེད་མང་རབ

༄༅། །འདུག །ཚ་གྱང་དགྱུལ་བའི་སྔག་བསྲལ་ཆེ་རབ་འདུག །
གདུག་པའི་མཆོན་ཆའི་སོ་ནི་རྟོ་རབ་འདུག །ད་ལྷའི་འོ་སྐོལ་སེར་སྣ་ཆེན་པོ་
ཚོ༔ །ཤི་ནས་ཡི་དགས་ཡུལ་དུ་སྐྱེ་རབ་འདུག །བགྱིས་སྐོམ་སྲག་བསྲལ་
དཔག་མེད་ཡོད་རབ་འདུག །འོ་སྐོལ་ཡུལ་གྱི་ཤེ་སྡང་ཆེན་པོ་ཚོ། །འཆི་
བའི་དུས་སུ་འཕབ་ཆོད་ཡུལ་དུ་སྐྱེ། །འཕབ་ཆོད་སྲག་བསྲལ་དཔག་མེད་
ཡོད་རབ་འདུག །འོ་སྐོལ་འདི་ནས་བཤས་འགོར་འདུག་མི་ཚོ། །ཤི་མ་
ཐག་ནས་དམྱལ་བའི་ཟངས་ནང་སྐྱེ། །སོད་སོད་རྒྱུབ་རྒྱུབ་བཙོ་རྡོ་བསྲེག
གསུམ་ནི། །ལོ་གྲངས་མང་པོར་སྲག་བསྲལ་མྱོང་རབ་འདུག །ཚ་གྱང་
སྲག་བསྲལ་མི་བཟོད་འོ་དོད་འབོད། །ཁྲག་གི་མཆི་མ་མིག་ནས་འབབ་
རབ་འདུག །འདི་ན་འདུག་པའི་མི་སྐྱ་ཐལ་བ་རྣམས། །དུད་འགྲོ་མང་པོའི་
བཤས་འགོར་མ་འདུག་ཅིག །དགྱུལ་ཟངས་ནང་དུ་འོ་བཀྱལ་ཆེ་རབ་
འདུག །བཟའ་ཚང་མི་དྲག་ནམ་མཁའི་སྤྲིན་དང་འདྲ། །ཟན་ཤག་འཕབ་
མོ་མང་པོ་མ་བྱེད་ཅིག །ད་ཡང་འཕབ་ཆོད་གནས་སུ་སྐྱེ་རབ་འདུག །ཆོ་
ནི་མི་ཐག་བར་སྐྱད་གྱོག་དང་འད། །མི་ཚེ་རིང་བསམ་སྲོག་པའི་ཁུར་པོ་
ཁྲ༔ །དམ་ཆོས་མི་སྒྲུབ་དགྱུལ་བ་རབ་གིས་སྒྲུབ། །རང་གིས་རང་ཉིད་
ཕུང་བ་ལ་རེ་ད། །ཆོར་རྟ་རྣས་མི་ཐག་རྟ་མགོའི་ཟེལ་བ་འད། །གྲོ་བུར་ཉི
མའི་བར་ཆད་ནམ་ཡོང་མེད། །གང་ཡོད་རན་པའི་མཆོད་སྦྱིན་རེམ་རེམ་
གྱིས༔ །ལོངས་སྤྱོད་མི་ཐག་སྐྲི་ལམ་འགྱུར་བ་འད། །སད་མ་ཐག་ཏུ་འཇའ་
ཚོན་བཞིན་དུ་ཡལ། །ཐམས་ཅད་མི་ཐག་པ་ཉེ་དེ་དང་མཚུངས། །མི་
ཐག་པ་ལ་ཐག་པར་འཛིན་མཁན་རྣམས། །རང་རྒྱུན་རང་ལ་རང་མགོ་རང

གིས་གཡོགས། །བཞད་ཕེང་གཏུབ་གསུམ་མནན་སྟེག་ཊབ་ཐོབ་ཊེད། །
མིག་གིས་མཐོང་བཞིན་བཙན་དུག་འགགས་པ་འདུ། །ཊན་པས་ཟིན་བཞིན་
ཀྱུལ་ལྟེབ་པ་འདུ། །ངོ་སྣོལ་འདིར་ཚོགས་མི་ལུས་ཐོབ་ཚད་ཚོ། །ལུས་
ཐོག་འདི་ལ་དགམ་ཚེས་མ་སྐྱབ་ན། །ཕྱིན་ཆད་མི་ལུས་ཐོབ་པ་བརྒྱ་ཆ་ཡིན། །
ཨེ་ཐོབ་མི་ཐོབ་རྒྱལ་ཁམས་ཡོངས་ལ་ལྟོས། །དི་རབ་ཆེན་པོ་དག་ལ་ཡར་
ལྟོས་དང་། །དི་དགས་སྒ་མིན་སྒ་ཚོགས་དུ་ཚམ་མཐོང་། །དབུ་ནག་མི་ཡི་
ལུས་འདི་དུ་ཚམ་མཐོང་། །མི་ལུས་ཨེ་ཐོབ་མི་ཐོབ་བསམ་བློ་ཐོངས། །
ལུང་ཆེན་ཁོག་དང་ཐང་ཆེན་དགྱིལ་ན་ལྟོས། །དུང་འགྲོ་ཀྲང་བཞི་དག་གི་
མང་ཉུང་དང་། །མི་ལུས་དགོན་མེད་བསམ་བློ་ཐོངས་དང་གསལ། །དབུར་
ཊ་གསུམ་དང་སྟོན་ཊ་གསུམ་པོ་ལ། །སྒྱང་སྟེང་རྟུ་གསེབ་ཀུན་ལ་ལྟོས་དང་
ནི། །དབུ་ནག་མི་དང་གྲངས་ཀ་སུ་མང་ལྟོས། །འདུ་སྲིན་རྣམས་ནི་སྐྱུ་ཚུབ་
ཉི་ལི་ལི། །ལས་འང་དབང་གིས་ལུས་འན་གྲངས་ཀ་མང་། །མགོ་ནག་མི་
ལུས་འདི་ནི་གྲངས་རེ་ཉུང་། །མཚོ་བསམ་གྱིས་དང་མི་ལུས་ཨེ་དགོན་རིག །
མཁར་ལ་འདབ་ཆགས་བྱ་རིགས་དུ་ཚམ་མཐོང་། །ཀྱུ་བོའི་གཞུང་ལ་འང་
ཕྱད་མོ་ལྟོས་དང་ནི། །ཊ་སྦྲལ་ལྟེང་གསུམ་ཀྱུ་བུའི་རིགས་རྣམས་ཀྱུང་། །
ལས་ཀྱི་དབང་གིས་ལུས་འན་དཔག་ཏུ་མེད། །གྲངས་མེད་བླངས་པའི་དུ་
འགྲོ་བློན་ཞིང་སྐྱགས། །སྐུ་མེད་དུང་འགྲོའི་རིགས་ལ་བསམ་མི་ཁྱབ། །སྐུ་
ཉེས་མི་ཡི་ལུས་འདི་དུ་ཚམ་མཐོང་། །དག་པ་མི་དང་མ་དག་དུང་འགྲོའི་
རིགས། །ཀྱུ་བུར་མིག་གི་ཡུལ་དུ་གང་མང་ལྟོས། །ནམ་མཁའི་བདག་པོས་
སྐུ་ཚོགས་སྟོན་པའི་ཡུལ། །ཀུན་བྱེད་རྒྱལ་པོ་ཟེར་བའི་བུ་ཆུང་ཞིག །ཀང་

༄༅། །གཉིས་སྦྱོར་པའི་རྩེ་མོའི་ཐེའུ་འཕྲུའི་སྟེང་། །ཚོ་རྟ་པ་ཡི་གུར་ཁྱིམ་པོ་ཕྲང་དབུས། །གསལ་སྟོང་སྤྲོན་མེ་ལྟ་བུའི་བུ་རྒྱུད་དེས། །གང་ནར་རོ་བོ་སྐུ་ཚོགས་རོལ་ཅིང་སྐྱོན། །དལ་འགྱུར་མི་ལུས་དཀོན་མོད་དེ་ལ་བརྗེས། །ཕྲང་གཅིག་ཊིས་པས་བཏད་རྒྱུ་མི་འདུག་ཀྱང་། །ཡང་ནས་ཡང་དུ་བརྗེས་དང་རྣལ་ད་ཡོད། །རིག་པའི་ཞི་འཁྱུ་རྒྱུན་བྱེད་རྒྱལ་པོ་འདི། །ཁྲིས་པ་ཡིན་པས་འཁྱུལ་པར་བདག་ཏུ་བཟུང་། །ཁྲིས་པ་མིན་པས་འཁོར་འདས་ཀུན་གྱི་གཞི། །དལ་འགྱུར་མི་ལུས་ལན་གཅིག་ཐོབ་དུས་འདིར། །མི་ཚེ་གཡེང་བ་སྟེག་པའི་ལས་ལ་འཛོམ། །ཕྲི་མར་ཕན་པའི་དམ་ཆོས་མ་སྒྲུབ་ན། །འཆི་ཚེ་ཚོར་བསོང་བགྱོད་དུས་ཡ་རེ་ང་། །དེ་ཕྱིར་སྤྲོས་ཞིག་རང་གི་སེམས་ལ་སྤྱོས། །སེམས་ཉིད་འདི་ལ་དངོས་པོར་གྲུབ་པ་མེད། །གྲུབ་པ་མེད་པའི་རོ་བོ་དེ་ལ་སྤྱོས། །སྐུ་ཚོགས་སྣང་བ་རོ་བོ་ཚོ་འཕྱལ་ཡིན། །ཚོ་འཕྱལ་བྱུང་ཡང་རོ་བོ་རང་ལས་བྱུང་། །ཚོ་འཕྱལ་ཐིམ་ཡང་རོ་བོ་རང་ལ་ཕྱིམ། །གཟུང་འཛིན་མེད་པ་རྒྱུན་དང་བླ་གཟུགས་ལྟར། །དངོས་པོ་ཅི་ཡང་མ་གྲུབ་སྟོང་པ་ཞིག །དན་བུ་དན་བྱེད་བཤགས་སོ་མེད་པ་དང་། །བཤག་ཡུལ་འཛོག་མཁན་གཉིས་སུ་མ་གྲུབ་ཀྱང་། །དན་པས་ཟིན་བཞིན་ས་ལེ་སིང་རེ་བ། །འདི་ཉིད་དངོས་པོ་གཤིས་ཀྱི་གནས་ལུགས་ཏེ། །བཟང་དན་གང་པར་དེ་ཡི་རོ་བོར་སྤྱོས། །ཅི་ལྟར་ཕར་ཡང་བཟོ་བཅོས་མི་བྱ་བར། །མ་བཅོས་སོ་མ་རང་བབ་ཉིད་དུ་ཞོག །མ་བཅོས་དེ་ཀར་འཛོག་པའི་ཏིང་ངེ་འཛིན། །དེའི་ཕྱག་རྒྱ་ཆེན་པོ་ཡིན་རབ་འདུག །ཡིན་རམ་མིན་རམ་སྣམ་པའི་ཐེ་ཚོམ་ནི། །མི་དགོས་པ་ནི་རྒྱལ་བས་གསུང་རབ་འདུག །ཡག་ཏུ་རེ

བ་ཉེས་ཀྱི་དོགས་པ་སྤོངས། །རིག་རིག་དྲན་དྲན་ཏུར་ཏུར་སྲ་ཚོགས་
གུན། །དྲན་རྟིས་ཟིན་བཞིན་རྒྱུན་དུ་སྐྱོང་བ་ན། །ཁང་ཤར་རང་གྲོལ་བདེ་
བ་ཆེན་པོ་ཉིད། །ཐག་བཅུས་དགེ་ཚོགས་བསྐྱལ་པར་བསགས་པ་བས། །
སྟོང་ཉིད་ཐུན་གཅིག་བསྐོམ་པ་བསོད་ནམས་ཆེ། །ཀུན་བཏགས་ཀློས་བྱས་
ཆོས་སྐྱོ་མཐའ་ཡས་ཀྱང་། །གནས་ལུགས་རང་ཞལ་མ་ཧོགས་དོན་རེ་
ཆུང་༎ །དེ་ཕྱིར་སྐྱིང་ནས་དམ་ཆོས་སྐྱབ་འདོད་རྣམས། །སྐྱད་མོ་ཡུལ་ལ་
མ་བལྟ་སེམས་ལ་ལྟོས། །ཁྱི་དོར་ལུས་ལ་མ་བྱེད་སེམས་ལ་གྱིས། །ཕྱི་ཡི་
སྣང་བའི་ཡུལ་ལ་ལྟོས་དང་ཉི། །སྣང་བ་འདི་དག་འཟིན་མེད་སྟོང་པ་ཉིད། །
བསྐུས་པས་མི་མཐོང་དོ་པོ་སྐྱོད་ལ་ཞིག །བཞག་པས་མི་འདུག་རྐང་མེད་
བྱིང་བཞིར་རྒྱུག །རྒྱུག་བྱེད་མཁན་པོའི་རང་གཟུགས་དེ་ལ་ལྟོས། །ཐག་
རིང་མི་འགྲོ་དང་གིས་རང་ལ་འཁོར། །དཔེར་ན་རྒྱ་མཚོ་ཆུ་ཡི་ཀྱུང་རྫ་
ནས༎ །ཉ་མོ་གསེར་མིག་མི་འདུག་ཀུན་ཏུ་རྒྱུག །རིང་པོར་མི་འགྲོ་རྒྱ་
མཚོའི་ནང་དུ་འཁོར། །ནད་གི་རིག་པ་དོ་པོའི་ཡུལ་དུ་ལྟོས། །ཀུན་བྱེད་
རྒྱལ་པོ་འདི་ཡིས་ཅི་བྱེད་ལྟོས། །བྱེད་རྒྱ་མང་པོ་ཁོ་ལ་ཡོད་པ་ཡིན། །
བཟང་པོའི་ཡོན་ཏན་སྲ་ཚོགས་ཁོ་ལས་འབྱུང་། །ངན་པ་སྐྱོན་གྱི་ཕྱག་ཀུན་
ཁོ་ཡིས་བཟུང་། །ཀུན་གྱི་ཅ་བ་རང་རིག་འདི་ཡིན། །ཡིན་པར་ཤེས་
བཞིན་སྐྱོང་ཉིད་སྟིང་རྗེའི་ཁམས། །ཟུང་དུ་འཟུག་པས་མ་ཧོགས་འགྲོ་བ་
ལ༎ །བཙས་མིན་ཕྱགས་འབྱུང་སྟིང་རྗེ་ཆེན་པོ་ཡིས། །བསྐོ་བྱ་བསྐོ་བྱེད་
བསྐོས་པ་མི་དམིགས་པ། །འཁོར་གསུམ་ཡོངས་སུ་དག་པས་རྒྱས་བཏབ་
སྟེ༎ །བླ་ན་མེད་པ་བྱང་ཆུབ་མཚོག་གི་གཞི། །སྣང་གྲགས་རྟོག་ཚོགས་ཡེ་

༄༅། །ནས་ཆོས་སྐུ་ཉིད། །ཡིན་པར་ཤེས་བཞིན་དེར་འཛིན་མེད་པ་
རྡོ། །ཆོགས་དྲུག་སྣང་བ་བྱུར་མེད་ལྷུག་པའི་དང་། །རང་རར་གྲོལ་ན་བདེ་
ཆེན་ཆོས་ཀྱི་སྐུ། །འདི་ནི་སངས་རྒྱས་དགོངས་པ་བླུན་མེད། །ཆོས་རྣམས་
ཀུན་གྱི་འགག་དོན་དྲིལ་བ་ཡིན། །མི་ཚེ་མི་རྟག་རྩྭང་གསེབ་མར་མེ་འདྲ། །
འཆི་བདག་བདུད་ནི་གྱིབ་སོ་གུག་པ་འདྲ། །འོ་སྐྱོལ་མི་རྟག་ལ་ཁའི་ཉི་མ་
འདྲ། །ཁོར་རྫས་མི་རྟག་རྩ་མགོའི་ཟིལ་པ་འདྲ། །ལོངས་སྤྱོད་མི་རྟག་ནམ་
མཁའི་སྤྲིན་དང་འདྲ། །བཟའ་ཆང་མི་རྟག་ཆོང་དྲུས་མགྲོན་པོ་འདྲ། །
གཉེན་རྗེའི་པོ་ན་རྣམ་མཁའི་ཕོག་དང་འདྲ། །བདུད་ཀྱི་བར་ཆད་གྲོ་བུར་ས་
ལྷར་གཡོ། །འོ་སྐྱོལ་འཇིག་རྟེན་མགོ་ནག་མི་རྣམས་ཉོན། །མི་གཅང་སྣ་
ལུས་ས་ཁྲག་ཤུང་པོ་འདི། །སྣ་མའི་ལུས་ཀྱི་ཁང་རྐྱེན་དམར་པོ་འདིར། །ཕྱི་
ནས་འཁྱགས་དོགས་དུང་འགྲོའི་པགས་པས་གཏུམས། །དེ་ལ་བཟང་
མདོག་དར་རས་འབུ་རྒྱུན་འཕེན། །ཨི་ཡག་མི་ཡག་སྤྲ་བསླུས་ཕྱི་ལྷ་བྱེད། །
ནང་ནས་སྤྱོགས་དོགས་ལང་ཚོ་ཟས་ཀྱིས་གསོ། །ཨི་ཞིམ་ཨི་སྲུག་གཡོ་
ལྷུགས་སྣ་ཆོགས་བྱེད། །ཞིམ་པའི་ཐབས་ལ་ས་རྫོ་མིན་པ་འདེབ། །དེ་
འདུའི་ལོངས་སྤྱོད་ཟས་ཀྱིས་ནང་ནས་གསོ། །ཕྱི་ནས་གཏུམས་ཤིང་ནང་
ནས་གསོས་པའི་ལུས། །སྤྲ་མ་ལུས་ཀྱི་ག་ཁྲག་ཁང་པ་འདི། །ཁང་རྐྱན་
བཞིན་དུ་རྣམ་རྗེབ་ཆ་མེད་པས། །དེ་རིང་ཉིད་ནས་ཆོས་ལ་བརྩོན་འགྲུས་
བསྐྱེད། །དམ་ཆོས་མི་སྒྲུབ་ལས་ངན་སྡིག་སྒྲུབ་ཚོ། །དེ་རིང་ཉིད་ནས་
བསམ་པ་ཆོས་ལ་གཏོད། །འཆི་བདག་བདུད་ཀྱི་བསུ་བ་ནམ་ཡོང་མེད། །
དེ་རིང་ཉིད་ནས་བློ་ཕུགས་ཆོས་ལ་གཏོད། །གཉེན་རྗེའི་པོ་ནའི་ཐག་པ་

ནམ་ཡོང་མེད། །དེ་རིང་ཉིད་ནས་བསམ་པ་ཆོས་ལ་གཏོད། །སྒྱུ་མའི་ལུས་
ལ་ནད་ཀྱིས་ནམ་ཟིན་མེད། །དེ་རིང་ཉིད་ནས་བསམ་པ་ཆོས་ལ་གཏོད། །
ནད་ཀྱིས་ཐེབས་ནས་ལུས་འདི་ནམ་འཇིག་མེད། །དེ་རིང་ཉིད་ནས་བསམ་
པ་ཆོས་ལ་གཏོད། །ལུས་ལ་གདོན་གྱི་གློ་བུར་ནམ་ཡོང་མེད། །དེ་རིང་ཉིད་
ནས་བསམ་པ་ཆོས་ལ་གཏོད། །འཆི་བའི་དུས་ན་རིགས་དྲུག་སྡུག་བསྔལ་
མྱོང་༔ །དེ་རིང་ཉིད་ནས་བསམ་པ་ཆོས་ལ་གཏོད། །རིགས་དྲུག་སོ་སོའི་
སྡུག་བསྔལ་བསམ་མི་ཁྱབ། །དེ་རིང་ཉིད་ནས་བསམ་པ་ཆོས་ལ་གཏོད། །
ཡུལ་སྡེ་ཆེན་པོའི་དཔོན་པོ་རྣམས་ཀྱིས་ཀྱང་། །ཁྲིམས་ཀྱི་ལ་ཞུགས་དམ་
པའི་ཆོས་ལ་གཏོད། །འདི་ཕྱི་གཉིས་ཡོད་ཡིན་པས་ཐུགས་དགོངས་
མཛོད༔ །ཁྲིམས་ལོག་བྱེད་ནས་དམོད་པ་མ་བསྡུ་ཞིག །བུད་མེད་མང་
པོས་ཞེ་ནད་བྱེད་ཅིང་དམོད། །ཚེ་འདིར་མི་དགེ་རྣམ་པ་སྣ་ཚོགས་འོང་། །
དེ་ལས་འོ་བརྒྱལ་ཆེ་ཞིག་ཕྱི་མར་འོང་། །ཁྲིམས་རྒྱ་ཆོས་དང་ལྡན་པས་
སྐྱབས་འགྲོ་འདུས། །འདི་ཕྱི་གཉིས་ཡོད་ཡིན་ནོ་ཐུགས་དགོངས་མཛོད། །
དེ་འོག་ཕྱི་བློན་ནང་བློན་བུ་ཚ་རྣམས། །དཔོན་གྱིས་མ་གསུངས་གསུངས་
ཟེར་མང་པོ་སླུ། །ན་ཚ་སྡུག་བསྔལ་དཔག་མེད་སྟེ་ལ་འདོན། །ཡོད་མེད་བླ་
བོ་ཡིན་མིན་ཟེར་ལོང་མེད། །ཕྱག་ཆ་ཀླད་ལ་བསྐོར་ནས་ཡོབ་རྗེབ་བྱེད། །
ཚུར་འོང་དཔོན་གྱི་དྲུང་དུ་ཕྱིན་པའི་ཚེ། །མ་ཞུས་ཞུ་བྱ་མང་པོ་ཞུལ་སྙད་
བྱེད༔ །དཔོན་གྱི་ཐུགས་དཀྲུགས་སྟེ་ལ་མྱ་ངན་འདོན། །དེ་འདྲ་མ་བྱེད་བུ་
ཚ་ཁྲལ་སྡུད་ཚོ། །བན་བོན་ཕལ་ཆེར་དག་ལ་འགྲུས་པ་བས། །སྡེ་ནག་
ཡོངས་ཀྱི་དམོད་ངན་འཇིགས་པར་བཤད། །བུད་མེད་མང་པོའི་དམོད་ངན་

༄༅། །དེ་དག་གིས། རྫོ་རྗེའི་ཕྱག་ཉིལ་རྒྱ་མཚོ་ཆེན་པོ་སྨྲ། ཚོ་
འདིར་མི་བདེ་སྲུག་བསྲལ་ནད་ཆེན་གྱིས། །ཐེབས་ཉེན་ཡོད་པས་དེ་འདུ་མ
བྱེད་ཅིག །ཕྱི་མ་དམྱལ་བའི་སྲུག་བསྲལ་ཆེན་པོ་ནི། །མི་ཚོ་ལོ་གངས་དུང་
ཕྱུར་སཱ་ལ། །བཅུ་བཟློག་ཆེན་པོའི་གནས་སུ་སྐྱེ་རབ་འདུག །དེ་འདུ
མ་བྱེད་བློ་ཕྱོགས་ཚོས་ལ་གཏོད། །དམ་པའི་ཚོས་ནི་བྱིན་རླབས་ཆེ་རབ
འདུག །རྒྱལ་ཁམས་ཡོངས་ཀྱི་ཕ་ཁུ་ཀུན་རབས་ཚོ། །བག་ཆགས་ངན་
པའི་སེམས་ཁྱར་མ་བྱེད་ཅིག །ཕྱི་མར་ཕན་པའི་དམ་ཚོས་སེམས་ཁྱར་
གྱིས། །སེམས་ཁྱར་བྱེད་རྒྱུའི་གོ་ས་མ་ཉོར་ཅིག །གོ་ས་ཉོར་ན་འདི་ཕྱི
གཉིས་མེད་འོང་། །བུ་དང་ཚོ་བོ་ཁྱིམ་ཚང་གང་ཡོད་ཀྱིས། །ཁ་ཚོས་ལོ་
གཡོག་མི་དགོས་དགོས་ཁར་བྱེད། །བློ་བུར་བར་ཆད་དུར་ཕུམ་ཕོག་ལྷར
ལྷུང་། །ཕྱི་རབས་རྗེས་འཇུག་རྣམས་ཀྱིས་ཕན་ལ་མེད། །ཡ་རབས་ཚོས
ལྷུན་རེ་རེ་མ་གཏོགས་ལ། །ཐན་པ་མེད་པ་དུས་ལོག་སྟོབས་ཀྱིས་ཡིན། །
ཡ་རབས་ཚོས་ལྷུན་རེ་རེ་ཡོད་པའི་མིས། །བཞིན་རས་དུན་ཅིང་སེམས་ལ
མི་བཟོད་པས། །ཡི་མུག་ཆེན་པོས་དགེ་རྩ་ཚོས་ལ་བསྐུལ། །དེ་འདུའི་མི
ནི་ཉིན་སྣར་ལས་ཀྱང་ཁུང་། །མི་ངན་དག་གིས་ཁག་གསུམ་སྟེང་ནས
བཟེད། །ཨི་རེད་མི་རེད་གཉེན་པོ་སྟོན་མར་ལྷོས། །ཡ་ང་བར་དོ་གཉེན
རྗེའི་ཡུལ་དུ་ནི། །ཡི་མུག་རང་ཉིད་གཅིག་ཕུར་འཁྱམས་པའི་དུས། །
གཉེན་དང་ཉེ་དུ་འགྲོ་རོགས་ཡོད་རབ་མེད། །བུ་དང་ཚོ་བོ་འཁྱམས་རོགས
ཡོད་རབ་མེད། །ལས་དབང་དགེ་སྡིག་འབྲས་བུས་སྟོན་ནས་སྐྱག །ལས
མཐན་འཆི་བདག་དགྲ་ཡིས་རྒྱབ་ནས་དེད། །ཤིག་གཅིག་བསད་ཀྱང་སྐྱང

སཱ་ཡོད་རབ་མེད། །དལ་འབྱོར་མི་ལུས་འདི་ཉིད་རྙེད་ཐོག་འདིར། །དཀར་
པོའི་དགེ་བར་བརྩོན་ཅིག་རིགས་ཀྱི་བུ། །ལ་ཁར་ཐོན་པའི་མ་ཕྱི་ཀྱུན་
རབས་རྣམས། །དུག་ལུ་འདོད་ཆགས་རྗེས་སུ་མ་འབྲང་ཞིག །བུད་མེད་
རིགས་འདི་གཡོ་དུག་ཤིན་ཏུ་ཆེ། །བུད་མེད་ཁ་ནི་མི་དགེའི་བང་མཛོད་
ཡིན༔ །བུ་བྱེད་མང་བས་བུད་མེད་འདི་དང་མཆུངས། །བུད་མེད་རིགས་
འདི་འདོད་ཆགས་ཆེ་རབ་འདུག །རབ་བྱུང་རྣམས་ཀྱི་སྐྱོམ་པ་ས་དང་
བསྲེ༔ །འདོད་ཆགས་ཐྲེག་བྱེད་ཕལ་མ་རེ་ལ་ནི། །ལོ་ནི་སྐྱོང་ཕྲག་རེ་ལ་
སྐྱེ་རབ་འདུག །སྐྱག་བསྐྱལ་མྱུ་ན་དཔག་མེད་ཤྱོང་རབ་འདུག །བུད་མེད་
རྣམས་ཀྱི་ལུས་དག་ཡིད་གསུམ་ལ། །མི་དགེ་རྣམ་པ་སྣ་ཚོགས་སེམས་ལ་
ཆང་༔ །ཆགས་པ་ཆེན་པོ་བུད་མེད་སེམས་ལ་ཆང་། །ཞེ་སྡང་ཆེན་པོ་བུད་
མེད་སེམས་ལ་ཆང་། །གཏི་མུག་ཆེན་པོ་བུད་མེད་སེམས་ལ་ཆང་། །ང་
རྒྱལ་ཆེན་པོ་བུད་མེད་སེམས་ལ་ཆང་། །ཕྲག་དོག་ཆེན་པོ་བུད་མེད་སེམས་
ལ་ཆང་། །སེར་སྣ་ཆེན་པོ་བུད་མེད་སེམས་ལ་ཆང་། །རྫུན་སེམས་ཟ་ཆེ་
བུད་མེད་སེམས་ལ་ཆང་། །ཉོན་མོངས་དུག་ལྔ་བུད་མེད་སེམས་ལ་ཆང་། །
སྐྱེ་བ་དམན་པའི་བུད་མེད་འདི་རྣམས་ཀྱིས། །ཅི་གོ་བཤད་ཅིང་ཅི་དྲན་
ཕྱག་པོར་སྒྱུར། །ཅི་རག་ཟ་ཞིང་ཅི་དྲན་བྱེད་དུ་འགྲོ། །ཡུལ་ཁམས་ཐམས་
ཅད་ཁ་ཕྱི་སྐྱོང་བས་དགུགས། །དོན་མེད་མི་ཡིས་མ་གཏུམ་གཏུམ་བར་
བཙུད༔ །དོན་དག་མེད་པའི་མནའ་དགེ་དགོད་བྱེད་སྐུབ། །དེ་འདྲ་མ་བྱེད་
ནག་ཆགས་བུད་མེད་རྣམས། །རྒྱལ་ཁམས་ཡོངས་ཀྱི་ཕོ་མོ་རྣས་པ་ཚོ། །
མི་ཚེ་ལོ་གྲངས་དུ་རེད་བསམ་བློ་ཐོངས། །རང་གི་ལོ་གྲངས་དུ་ཉི་དུ་ལུས

༄༅། །སློས། །དའི་འཆི་རན་ཡིན་ནོ་བསམ་དྲོ་ཐོངས། །ཁྲིམ་ཚང་
གང་ཡོད་གཞན་པ་དེ་རྣམས་ཀྱི། །སེམས་རྒྱུད་དགུགས་ཤིང་མནན་དགེ་མ་
སྐྱབས་ཤིག །སྐྱབ་རྒྱུ་ཅི་བྱུང་དག་པའི་ལྷ་ཚོགས་སྐྱབས། །ཁ་ནས་ཡིག
དྲག་ལག་གིས་འབོར་ལོ་བསྐོར། །སེམས་ལ་འཆི་བ་མི་རྟག་སྟེང་ནས་
སྐོམས༔ །རང་གི་ལོ་གྲངས་མཉམ་པའི་ཉེ་དུ་ལས། །དུ་ཚམ་འདུག་དང་
དུ་ཚམ་ཤི་ཟིན་སྐོས། །མི་རྟག་པ་ལ་རྟག་སྙམ་བྱེད་པ་འཁྲུལ། །འཁྲུལ་པ་
ཅུད་ནས་ཆོད་ཅིག་རྣས་པ་ཚོ༔ །དག་སྣང་ཕྱོགས་མེད་ཀྱིས་ཤིག་རྣས་པ་
ཚོ༔ །འཆི་བ་སྙིང་ནས་སྐོམས་ཤིག་རྣས་པ་ཚོ། །བླ་མ་སྒྱི་བོར་སྐོམས་
ཤིག་རྣས་པ་ཚོ། །དགོང་འཁའི་ཉི་མ་འདི་ལ་ཡར་ལྟོས་དང་། །ཉི་མ་ཐར་ས་
ཉེ་དང་འགྲིབ་སར་ཉེ། །བསམ་དྲོ་ཐོངས་དང་རྣས་པ་འཁྲུལ་བ་ཚོ། །རྣས་
པ་མི་རྟག་ལ་ཁའི་ཉི་མ་འདུ། །སྐྱིང་གཏམ་ཡིན་ནོ་རྣས་པ་ཕོ་མོ་ཚོ། །འཆི་
བདག་བདུད་ཀྱིས་སྒྲོ་རྒྱག་ནམ་ཡོང་མེད། །རྣས་གཞན་མེད་པས་དམ་ཆོས་
སྙིང་ནས་འབད། །སེམས་ལ་ཞིག་དང་སྙིང་གི་བླུ་བོ་ཡིན། །ཡང་གཅིག
གསོན་དང་ཡིན་བདག་བསོད་རྣམས་འཕེལ། །སློ་མ་པ་རྗེ་རྗེའི་ཚོས་བརྒྱུད་
རིགས་ཀྱི་བུ། །རལ་པ་ཁམས་འབེབས་རིགས་བརྒྱུད་བསོད་རྣམས་
འཕེལ༔ །བསགས་པ་ལམ་ལོག་མ་ཕོར་དམ་ཆོས་སྐྱབས། །ཞེས་
གསུངས་སོ། །ཡིན་བདག་བསོད་རྣམས་འཕེལ་གྱིས་ཞུས་པ། བདག་ལ་
བསགས་པ་ཆེན་པོ་ཡོད་ཀྱང་དོན་མེད་དུ་འགྲོ་བར་འདུག །ང་ལ་བུ་གཅིག
ཡོད་པ་འདི་ནི་གཟའ་པོ་ཁྲི་ལས་བྱེད་པ་ཞིག་འདུག་པས་ང་རེ་སྐྱག །ད་ནི་
ང་ཡིས་བསགས་པ་ལ་འདི་རྣམས་དམ་པའི་ལྷ་ཚོས་ཞིག་གི་རྒྱ་བར་བསམ་

ལགས༔    དེད་ཀྲས་པ་ཕོ་མོ་རྣམས་ལ་མི་དྲག་པའི་མགུར་དང་ཚོས་ཐུན་དེ་
རྣམས་བགའ་དྲིན་ཆེའོ། །ང་རའི་བསགས་པ་འདིས་སྨ་འགྲོ་རྟེན་བཞིངས་
ཤིག་བསམ་པས་ཚོས་གང་བཞིངས་དང་གཞན་པ་ཕོ་མོ་ལའང་ཚོས་སྐྱལ་མ་
ཆད་ཙམ་ཞུ་ཞིས་ཞུས་པས།    བྱ་མའི་ཞལ་ནས་འདི་སྐྱད་ཅེས་གསུངས་
སོ༔  །ཡང་གཅིག་གསོན་དང་རལ་པ་ཁམས་འབེབས་བཀྲུད། །
ཁྱོད་ཀྱིས་བསགས་པའི་སྨ་འགྲོ་རྟེན་བཞིངས་ནི། །དམ་པ་བཅུ་གཉིས་གོ་
ཕྲེས་བྱུས་ན་ལེགས། །དེ་ནས་ཙི་འདོད་མདོ་སྩུ་དུ་བཞིངས་ཀྱིས། །འདིན་
འདུས་པའི་ཕོ་མོ་གཞན་པ་ཚོ། །རང་ལུས་དར་ལ་བབ་པའི་ཕོ་མོ་རྣམས། །
ཕ་མ་ཀྲན་རྟོན་འདྲེ་རུ་མ་མཐོང་ཞིག །ཕ་མ་བླ་མ་སྒྲོབ་དཔོན་འདི་གསུམ་
ནི༔ །འདྲེ་རུ་མཐོང་ནས་ལོག་ལྟ་སྐྱེས་པ་ཡིས། །མནར་མེད་དམྱལ་བ་དག་
ལ་སྐྱེ་རབ་འདུག །ཕ་མ་མེས་པོ་ཚུན་ཀྱིས་བསགས་པ་དེ། །འདི་ཡིན་ཟེར་
ཞིང་ལེ་བསྐྱེད་གང་ཕོག་བྱེད།    །སྤུར་ཀྱི་བསགས་མཁན་ཕ་མ་དེ་རྣམས་
ཀྱང་༔  །སྒྲོག་རྡལ་བཞིན་དུ་གཏུ་ལྷག་མར་ལ་བོར། །རྒྱུ་འདི་ངས་
བསགས་ཟེར་ཞིང་སྨ་ལོག་སྒྱུར།   །ཕྱིན་ཀྱི་བསགས་མི་ཕ་མ་དེ་རྣམས་
ཀྱིས༔ །མ་གའི་གདུ་ནས་ཡར་ལ་ཙི་བྱེད་ལྷ། །ཡིན་མིན་བླ་བོ་ཚོག་རུར་
འཆར་ཚམ་ནས། །བྲི་ཀྲན་རོ་ཀྲན་སྐྱད་སྐྱ་མ་གོ་ཟེར། །མི་རུང་བ་ཡི་ལུང་
འདྲེན་སྨ་ཚོགས་བྱེད། །དྲིན་ཅན་ཕ་མ་བླ་མ་སྒྲོབ་དཔོན་ལ། །ངན་པ་དག་
གིས་ལུང་འདྲེན་གང་བྱས་དེས། །ལུས་ངན་དེ་འདྲའི་སྐྱེ་བ་ལྷ་བརྒྱ་ལེན། །
བར་མཚམས་དམྱལ་བའི་སྡུག་བསྔལ་མང་པོ་མྱོང་། །དེ་འདྲ་བྱེད་གཞན་
པ་ཕོ་མོ་རྣམས། །དྲིན་ཅན་ཕ་མ་བླ་མ་སྒྲོབ་དཔོན་གསུམ། །མཚོད་པའི་

120

༄༅། །ཞིང་ས་ཡིན་པ་རྒྱལ་བས་གསུངས། །ལང་ཚོ་དང་ལ་བབ་པའི་
ཕོ་མོ་རྣམས། །མང་པོ་བཞད་ཀྱང་གོ་བར་མི་འདུག་པས། །དཔ་པའི་ཚོས་
ཀྱི་སྙིང་གཏམ་ཐིག་པ་འདི། །འཇིག་རྟེན་གཏམ་གྱི་དཔེ་ལ་མི་ཐབ་རྒྱས། །
མདོ་རྒྱུད་ཀུན་ནས་རེ་ལྷར་བཞད་ལགས་ཀྱང་། །བསྐལ་བ་སྙིགས་མའི་
འཇིག་རྟེན་ཕོ་མོ་ཚོས། །གོ་རྒྱུ་མེད་དེ་འཇིག་རྟེན་བཞག་པ་ཡིན། །མ་ཡིན་
འཁྲུལ་གཏམ་འདུག་ན་བཟོད་པར་གསོལ། །འཇིག་རྟེན་མི་རྣམས་ཀུན་གྱི་
ཕྱེད་ལྷགས་ལ། །འཆི་རྒྱུ་མེད་པའི་འདུག་ས་ཡོད་པ་འདྲ། །བར་དོ་ཟེར་
བའི་འགྲོ་ས་མེད་པ་འདྲ། །དམྱལ་བ་ཟེར་བའི་འཇིགས་ས་ས་མེད་པ་འདྲ། །
དགེ་སྡིག་ཟེར་བའི་འབྲས་བུ་མེད་པ་འདྲ། །ཚོས་རྒྱལ་ཟེར་བའི་རྒྱལ་པོ་
མེད་པ་འདྲ། །ལས་མཁན་ཟེར་བའི་ སྟོན་པོ་མེད་པ་འདྲ། །ཁྲི་མདུང་ཟེར་
བའི་མཆོན་ཆ་མེད་པ་འདྲ། །ལྕགས་སྲེག་ཟེར་བའི་ཐང་ཆེན་མེད་པ་འདྲ། །
གཤིན་ལ་ཟེར་བའི་གཟར་མོ་མེད་པ་འདྲ། །གཤིན་ཐང་ཟེར་བའི་ཆེན་པོ་
མེད་པ་འདྲ། །ཆ་དམྱལ་ཟེར་བའི་ཚ་དང་མེད་པ་འདྲ། །གྲང་དམྱལ་ཟེར་
བའི་གྲང་དང་མེད་པ་འདྲ། །ཐིག་ནག་ཟེར་བའི་དམྱལ་བ་མེད་པ་འདྲ། །
བསྐུས་འཇོམས་ཟེར་བའི་དམྱལ་ཁམས་མེད་པ་འདྲ། །ལྕགས་ཁང་ཟེར་
བའི་ཁང་ཆུང་མེད་པ་འདྲ། །བཙོ་རྡོ་བྱེད་སའི་དམྱལ་ཟངས་མེད་པ་འདྲ། །
ཁྲོ་ཆུ་བོལ་བའི་ཞུན་མ་མེད་པ་འདྲ། །ལས་དན་བར་དོར་འཁྱམས་པའི་
སེམས་ཅན་རྣམས། །སྒྱུལ་ནག་ཞགས་པས་མགུལ་ནས་འཆེང་ཞིང་ཁྲིད། །
ཐོག་དང་སེར་བའི་དྲག་ཆར་ནན་དུ་ནི། །རང་དབང་མེད་པར་གཅེར་བུར་
ལག་སྟོང་དུ། །ས་ཕྱོགས་དེ་ན་འགྲོ་དགོས་མེད་པ་འདྲ། །རང་ཁྱིམ་འདི་

ན་འདུག་ས་ཡོད་པ་འདྲ། །རེ་འཕྲུལ་རེ་འཕྲུལ་འཇིག་རྟེན་མི་རེ་འཕྲུལ། །
རེ་སྨུག་རེ་སྨུག་འཇིག་རྟེན་མི་རེ་སྨུག །བསམ་བློ་བཏང་ན་སྨུག་འཕྲུལ་
གཉིས་ཀ་འཛོམ། །དེ་དག་མི་ཤེས་འཇིག་རྟེན་ཕལ་པ་སྟོ། །བློ་བས་
མི་ཆེད་ཕྱེབ་ཀྱིར་འགྲོ་བར་འདུག །དཔྱལ་ཁམས་བཅུ་བཅུད་བརྫོད་མེད་
སྨུག་བསལ་ཡོད། །དེ་འདྲའི་གནས་སུ་འདི་ནས་ཡིད་གིས་ཕྱེབ། །ད་ལྟ་
འཇིག་རྟེན་འདི་ན་འདུག་པའི་དུས། །འདི་ན་ཕྱེབ་ཟེར་མཐོང་རྒྱུ་མི་འདུག
སྟེ། །ལས་ཀྱི་དབང་གིས་ལུས་འདི་ཐུལ་མ་ཐག །རྣམ་སྨིན་ལས་དབང་
དག་པོས་ཕྱེབ་ནས་འགྲོ། །དེ་འདུ་ཡོད་མེད་ཐེ་ཚོམ་དགོས་རབ་མེད། །ཁོ་
བར་མཛོད་ཅིག་འདིར་ཚོགས་དང་ལྷུན་རྣམས། །བླ་མའི་བྱིན་རླབས་སྙིང་ལ་
འཇུག་པར་ཤོག །ཅེས་གསུངས་པ་ལ། ཡང་བུ་སྟོབ་རྣམས་ཀྱིས་ཞུས་པ།
དམ་པ་ཉིད་ཀྱིས་དུས་གསུམ་ཡོངས་སུ་མཁྱེན་པས་སྐྱར་ཡང་འོངས་འགྲོ་
བའི་དོན་དུ་ཡུང་བསྟན་ཞལ་ཆེམས་མདོར་བསྡུས་ཤིག་ཞུ་ཞེས་ཞུས་པས།
བླ་མའི་ཞལ་ནས། ཡང་གཅིག་གསོན་དང་སྐལ་ལྡན་ཁྱེད་རྣམས་ཉོན། །
ཁར་ཉིན་སྟེའུ་རྫ་བའི་ཆོས་བཅུ་ལ། །དཀི་འོད་གསལ་ཁོར་ཡུག་གནས་
པའི་ཆེ། །ཟངས་མདོག་དཔལ་རིའི་གནལ་ཡས་ཕོ་བྲང་ནས། །འཇའ་འོད་
ལྷ་ལྷུན་དར་གྱི་ཐག་པ་དེ། །ཁའོ་སྣང་བ་ཆོས་སྐུའི་མེ་ལོང་ལ། །དར་སྐུད་
འཐེན་པ་བཞིན་དུ་རང་ལ་རྫག །འཇའ་འོད་པདྨ་སྟོང་ལྡན་ཟེའུ་འབྲུའི
སྟེང་། །འོད་ཕྱུང་འབར་བའི་ཧྲྀཿཡིག་དཀར་པོ་གཅིག །ཉི་མ་འབུམ་
གྱི་གཟི་བརྗིད་ལྷུན་པ་སྲུང་། །འཕྲུལ་སྣང་སྐྱེ་ལམ་གང་ཡིན་བསམ་ནས་
ཀྱང་། །དེ་ལ་མ་ཡེངས་དྲན་རིག་ཡུང་ཚམ་བཞེ། །དེ་མ་ཐག་ཏུ་པར་

༄༅། །འབྱུང་གྱུར་ནས་ཀྱང་། །འཁོར་དུ་རིག་འཛིན་ཕོ་མོའི་ཚོགས་
ཀྱིས་བསྐོར། །ཁྱད་བསྟན་འདི་རྣམས་ཉམས་སྣང་ཡུལ་དུ་གསུངས། །མ
ཡིངས་གསོན་དང་གྲུབ་ཐོབ་རྡོ་རྗེ་འཛིན། །དུས་དང་སྟེགས་མ་སྲུམ་ཙུ་ཁ
རལ་དུས། །བོད་ཁམས་བདེ་བ་སྐྱད་ཅིག་མི་འབྱུང་ཞིང་། །ལོ་རེ་བཞིན་དུ
ནད་མཚོན་མུ་གེ་ནི། །ཁ་བ་བབས་བབ་བུ་ཡུག་འཁྱབས་འཁྱབ་བྱེད། །
སེམས་ཅན་མང་པོ་མུ་གིས་ལོ་བརྒྱལ་གཏད། །ནད་སྣ་མི་གཅིག་ཡམས་ནད
མང་པོ་འབྱུང་། །བོད་ཁམས་མི་ལ་བདེ་བ་མི་སྲིད་པས། །བན་བོན་ནང
འཁྲུག་ནང་སྐྱས་བརྟེག་ཐིག་བྱེད། །དེ་ཡང་བོད་ཁམས་འཁྲུག་པའི་སྲ་ལྷས
ཡིན༔ །ཡུལ་འདིར་བཀྲགས་ཤིང་ས་འདིར་གནས་པ་ཡི། །སར་གནས
བྱང་ཆུབ་སེམས་དཔའ་རྒྱབ་ཏུ་འཕེན། །ཕྱི་འདྲེ་ནང་འདྲུག་སེར་སྟུན་དང
དུ་ལེན། །དེ་ཡང་བོད་ཀྱི་བསྟན་པ་སྲ་ཉམས་དགགས། །འཛིག་རྟེན་མི
ནག་ཕོ་མོ་འདི་རྣམས་ཀྱིས། །རང་ཡུལ་བླ་དགོ་ཁྲི་བཞིན་ཡིད་ཀྱིས་བོར། །
ཕྱི་རོལ་ནང་འཁྲམས་རྟེན་པ་འགའ་ཞིག་འབྱུང་། །ཟབ་ཆོས་མང་པོ་ཁོ
ཡིས་སློང་བཤད་བྱེད། །སྐྱ་མའི་ནོར་གྱིས་ལབ་རྒྱ་མེད་དོ་སྐྲད། །དེ་སྐྲད
ཟེར་བའི་ཏོ་ཧྲུན་དང་དུ་ལེན། །དང་དུ་ལེན་ཅིང་ཡིད་ཀྱིས་ཏིང་ངེ་འཛིན། །
དེ་ཡང་བོད་ཀྱི་བསྟན་པ་ཉམས་དགགས་ཡིན། །བྱང་ཕྱོགས་གཉེན་ཆེན་ཐང
ལྷའི་བུ་མོ་ནི། །དགྲ་ལྷ་ཝེ་ཀར་རྒྱལ་པོས་རྒྱུང་མར་བླངས། །རིན་དང་རྫོང
འདེབས་ནད་དང་མཚོན་གྱིས་བྱེད། །དེ་ཡིས་སེམས་ཅན་མང་པོའི་བརྒྱལ
གཏད༔ །དེ་ཡི་དུས་སུ་ལྷ་འདྲེ་ཁ་དང་བས། །ལྷ་འདྲེ་དམ་ལོག་མི་མ་ཡིན
རྣམས་ཀྱིས། །གཙུག་ལག་ལག་ཁང་དང་དགེ་འདུན་ཚོགས་གྲལ་དགུགས། །

123

ཤུས་སྐྱེང་འདོས་སྐྱེང་མེད་པའི་ཁ་ཕྱེས་དགུགས། །འཛིང་རྒྱབ་འབོན་དང་
ཕྱེབ་རྒྱག་འཛིགས་ཁ་བགྱི། །སློན་ལམ་བདེན་ཚིག་རྣམས་ལ་བར་དུ
གཅོད། །དེ་འདུའི་དུས་སུ་བད་འབྱུང་ང་ཡིས་སློབ། །ཕྱུགས་རྗེ་ཆེན་པོའི
སྐྱལ་བ་མཆུའི་མིང་། །ཞིང་ཁམས་འདི་ནས་འོག་མིན་གཤེགས་ཚ་ན། །
དམ་སྲི་ཀ་ལ་དམར་མོ་མི་ལ་ཟོན། །བོད་ཀྱི་བསྟན་པ་མཐའ་རིའི་ཟོག་ནས
དགུགས། །སངས་རྒྱས་བསྟན་པའི་སྒྲོག་ཤིང་མང་པོ་གཅོད། །དེ་ནི་གི་དེ
ཀུ་ཡི་སྐྱལ་པ་ཡིན། །བ་སྒྲ་རེ་ལ་བདུད་བློན་སྐྱལ་པ་རེས། །སྐྱོང་སྐྱོང་སྐྱལ
པས་བོད་ཁམས་ས་སྟེང་ཁྱབ། །ཁ་ལ་དགེ་བཞེས་ཚ་བྱད་མད་རྒྱུད
དགུགས། །ཁ་ལ་རྒྱལ་པོའི་ཚ་བྱད་བོད་ཁམས་དགུགས། །ཁ་ལ་མི
དཔོན་ཚ་བྱད་ཡུལ་ཁམས་དགུགས། །ཁ་ལ་བློན་པོའི་ཚ་བྱད་སྲེ་ནག
དགུགས། །ཁ་ལ་མི་ནག་ཚ་བྱད་ཕ་ཚན་དགུགས། །ཁ་ལ་སེར་མོའི་ཚ
བྱད་དགོན་སྟེ་དགུགས། །ཁ་ལ་གྲུ་པའི་ཚ་བྱད་གྲུ་སློབ་དགུགས། །ཁ་ལ
ན་ཆུང་ཚ་བྱད་གྲོང་ཡུལ་དགུགས། །ཁ་ལ་བྱད་མེད་ཚ་བྱད་སྟེ་གཉིས
དགུགས། །དེ་ལྟར་མི་འདོད་སྣ་ཚོགས་དགུ་དགུགས་བྱེད། །དེ་རྣམས
བསྟན་བཤིག་བདུད་ཀྱི་བ་སྒྲ་ཡིན། །བདུད་ཀྱི་སྐྱལ་པ་དམར་པོ་མི་ལ
ཟོན།། །ཁྱག་ན་མེ་ཡི་མཚོན་ཚ་དར་མ་ཕོགས། །མི་སྲུག་གཟུགས་བཅུན
ཁྱི་ནག་རོལ་དུ་ཁྲིད། །ཚིག་ནི་མི་སྐྲན་ཁྱི་སྐད་ལན་གསུམ་རྣག །ཕན་སྐྱལ
ཀུ་ལའི་ཙོ་ཏྲ་ཕགས་ཀྱིས་འགས། །དེ་ནི་རབ་ཏུ་གས་པའི་སྟེང་ཁྲག་དེ། །
ས་ནི་དོང་མོའི་སྟེང་དུ་མེར་ཀྱིས་འཕྱིལ། །སྐྲང་རིགས་མི་གཉིག་མཐའ་པོ་གྲི
དུ་འཁེ། །ག་ཤེད་དང་དེ་རྣས་བོད་ཁམས་ཀུན་ལ་ཁྱབ། །བོད་ཡུལ་ཕམས

༄༅། །ཅན་ནད་དང་མུ་གེ་ནི། །རྒྱུང་ལྤར་འཆུབས་ཤིང་མྱུན་འཐིབ་ལྟ་
བུར་འོང་། །སྐྱེ་འགྲོ་སེམས་ཅན་མང་པོ་དུས་མིན་འཆི། །ལོ་ཉེས་སད་སེར་
མི་འདོད་རྫུང་ལྤར་འཆུབས། །མི་རྣམས་ཀུན་ལ་མི་འདོད་སྡུ་དགུ་འབྱུང་། །
དེ་འདྲའི་དུས་ངན་ཐ་མ་ཤར་བའི་ཚེ། །མི་ཕྱུགས་དག་ལ་གྲོ་བུར་བར་ཆད་
ཀྱིས། །མི་རོ་རོག་རོ་ལམ་ཁའི་རྫོ་བཞིན་དུ། །གོམ་རེ་བོར་མཆམས་
ཕོག་ཆགས་རེ་རེ་འཆི། །ཐར་གས་ངེད་ཆང་ཅི་ཡིན་ཅི་ཡིན་ཟེར། །ཆུང་
གས་ངེད་ཆང་ཅི་ཡིན་ཅི་ཡིན་ཟེར། །ཅི་ཡང་མ་ཡིན་གཤེད་ཀ་གདོན་ཕྲོག
ཡིན། །རྒྱལ་ཁམས་འཁྲུགས་པ་བྱས་པའི་གཤེད་ཁ་ཡིན། །ཕྲོགས་
གཉིས་སྟེ་འཁྲུགས་བྱས་པའི་གདོན་ཕྲོག་ཡིན། །ས་བདག་གདུག་པའི་སྙིང་
ཚལ་ཕྱི་ལ་ཕྱུང་། །དེ་ཉིད་ཁྲོས་པས་ཡུལ་ལ་ནད་ཡམས་གཏོང་། །ནད་ཁ་
ཡམས་ཁ་ཕལ་ཆེར་རང་གིས་ཉེས། །ངེད་ཆང་ཕྱི་གོང་བརྐུག་གསུམ་ཅི་ཡིན་
ཟེར། །དེའི་གཅིག་ལ་མ་ཡིན་ཀུན་ལ་ཡིན། །དེ་རྣམས་འདུལ་བའི་
ཐབས་ནི་ཅི་དྲག་ཞུས། །གསུང་རབ་རྣམས་ནི་ཅི་ཕོན་གསེར་དང་འདྲ། །
སྒྱུ་ལྤན་དག་གི་རབ་ཏུ་བྱུང་བ་ཡིས། །གསུང་རབ་བཀླགས་ན་སྒྱུ་འགྱུར་
བཞི་འགྱུར་ཡིན། །ཡུལ་ལུགས་དག་དང་མཐུན་པའི་སྒྱུང་བསྐྱེད་ཀྱིས། །
དེ་ནས་པརྟ་ང་ཉིད་དག་ཏུ་ཞོས། །གྲ་ར་ཁྲག་འཐུང་འབར་བའི་ལྟ་ཚོགས་
རྣམས། །ཕྱི་ནང་གསང་གསུམ་དག་པོའི་སྒྲུབ་པ་ནི། །གཏེར་ཁ་རེ་ལ་དྲག
སྒྲུབ་རེ་རེ་ཡོད། །དམར་ཆེན་གཏོར་མའི་དྲག་བཟློག་ཡང་ཡང་ཐུན། །བྱུང་
པར་སྣུས་ཡུལ་ལུང་པའི་སྟོང་ཕྱོགས་ན། །བྲག་དཀར་དུང་སེང་གནམ་ལ་
འཆོངས་འདུ་ཡོད། །དེ་འདྲའི་གནས་སུ་གཏེར་གྱི་ཡང་སྟེང་ཡོད། །དེ་དག

ཆོས་བདག་ལས་ཅན་ཁྱེད་རང་ཡིན། །དུས་ངན་སྙིགས་མར་རྟེན་འབྲེལ་
ཆོང་བར་དཀའ། །རྟེན་འབྲེལ་འཕྲུང་ནས་གདེང་གི་སྙིང་པོ་ཡིན། །ཐབ་
གཏེར་གསང་སྔགས་ཟབ་མོའི་ཡང་སྙིང་དེས། །འགྲོ་དོན་དཔག་མེད་
ཕྱོགས་དུས་ཀུན་ཏུ་ཁྱབ། །གཏེར་སྟོན་བརྫུའི་མིང་ཅན་དེ་དག་གིས། །
རྟེན་འཕྲེལ་གནད་ལ་བར་ཆད་མ་བྱུང་ན། །འགྲོ་དོན་ཆེ་ཕྱིར་སྣུས་གསང་དེ།
ཡིས་བརློག །སྟོང་ཉིད་བརློག་པས་ཉེ་དུ་ཀ་ཡང་བརློག །དེ་འདྲའི་བརློག་
པ་འདིག་རྟེན་འདི་ན་མེད། །དི་རབ་འབར་བའི་སྟེང་ནས་བརློག་པར་
འགྱུར། །དེ་འདྲའི་ཆོས་བདག་ལས་ཅན་ཁྱེད་རང་ཡིན། །བར་ཆད་ཆེ་
བས་དེ་ཡི་འགྲོ་དོན་དཀའ། །དེ་འདྲའི་དུས་སུ་ཁྲོ་རྒྱལ་ཡང་བརློག་ནི། །
བགའ་བརྒྱད་དགོངས་འདུས་ཕུར་པ་ལ་སོགས་པ། །ཀྱུ་རུ་དུག་པོའི་རིགས་
ལ་ཕྱི་ནང་དང་། །གསང་བ་གསུམ་དང་གཏེར་ཁ་གང་ཡོད་སོགས། །བླ་མ་
དུག་པོའི་གཏོར་བརློག་ཆད་བསྐུལ་དང་། །འཇམ་དཔལ་གཤིན་རྗེའི་ལྷ་
ཆོགས་དམར་ནག་དང་། །ཧྲུ་མཆོག་རོལ་པ་དམར་ནག་ལྷ་ཆོགས་དང་། །
ཕུག་རྟེར་ལ་སོགས་དུག་པོའི་གཏོར་བརློག་དང་། །ཁྲོས་ནག་མེད་གདོང་
མ་རྒྱུད་གཏོར་བརློག་སོགས། །ཐམས་ཅད་ཡིས་མ་བཅུམས་གང་ཡང་
མེད། །དེ་རྣམས་གང་གིས་བརློག་པར་བྱེ་ཆོམ་མེད། །སིརྩི་ཉིན་རྒྱུན་
མཆན་རྒྱན་མང་པོས་བརློག །དམ་ཆོས་རྟོགས་ཆེན་ཡུམ་ཆེན་པར་ཕྱིན་
དང་། །ཁྲི་རྒྱལ་འབར་བའི་གཏོར་བརློག་དུག་པོ་དང་། །བརློག་འབུམ་
ཁ་སྟོང་རི་རབ་མགོ་སྙིང་བརློག །ཤེས་རབ་སྟིང་པོ་ཁྲི་འདོན་བརློག་པ་
དང་། །གཅུག་གཏོར་སྟོང་བརློག་བདུ་འབུམ་བརློག་དང་། །སིརྩིའི་དར་

༄༅། །ཕྱུག་ཆེན་པོ་ཕྱུགས་པཞིར་ཆུགས། །ལྷོ་སྐུག་རྫ་སྐུག་བརྫོག་
པར་ཐེ་ཚོམ་མེད། །དེ་རྣམས་མི་རིགས་པོ་མོའི་སྙི་རིམ་ཡིན། །དུད་འགྲོ་
ཀྱང་བཞི་དག་གི་སྙི་རིམ་ལ། །ས་བདག་དང་ཞི་གཏོར་མ་འཐུམ་ཚོ་དང་། །
བསང་དང་ཞི་བ་གཞི་བདག་དཀར་གཏོར་དང་། །སྒྱུད་ནི་བརྒྱ་རྩ་ལ་སོགས་
སྙིན་པ་ཕོངས། །ཞོར་གཟུངས་གདུགས་དཀར་གཡང་སྐྱབས་ལ་སོགས་
པའི༔ །ཆབ་གཏོར་སྟོང་རྩ་ལ་སོགས་ཕོན་ན་ལེགས། །ཡང་གཅིག་གསོན་
དང་གྱུབ་ཕོབ་རྡོ་རྗེ་འརྫིན། །པདྨང་ཡིས་ཕྱི་རབས་བསྐྱ་བ་མེད། །རྒྱ་གར་
ཡུལ་གྱི་དམ་པ་སངས་རྒྱས་དང་། །ཞངས་རི་མཁར་དམར་མ་གཅིག་ལབ་
ཀྱི་སྒྲོན། །སྒྲོན་ལམ་དབང་གིས་འགྲོ་དོན་གཅིག་ཏུ་གྱུར། །རིག་པའི་རྩལ་
རྫོགས་སེམས་ཉིད་གཞི་རྩ་གཅོད། །འཁོར་བའི་གཞི་རྩ་གཅོད་པའི་གཅོད༔
ཆོགས་བྱུང་། །སེམས་ཉིད་གནས་ལུགས་གཅོད་པའི༔ །གཟུང་འཛིན་རྟོག
པ་གཅོད་པའི༔ །བདག་འཛིན་རྩ་བ་གཅོད་པའི༔ །དགྲ་གཞེན་གཅིག
ཐག་གཅོད་པའི༔ །བདེ་སྡུག་སྣང་བ་གཅོད་པའི༔ །གཅང་སྡེའི་རྣམ་རྟོག
གཅོད་པའི༔ །རི་དྭགས་གཅིག་ཏུ་གཅོད་པའི༔ །ལྟ་འདུ་རང་སེམས་
གཅོད་པའི༔ །རང་སེམས་དོ་བོ་གཅོད་པའི་གཅོད་ཆོགས་བྱུང་། །དེ་ལྟར་
གཅོད་ཀྱི་ཆོགས་འཁོར་ཆེན་པོ་འདི། །འགྲོ་ཀུན་རྒྱུན་རྒྲོག་འདི་ལས་ཟབ
པ་མེད། །ཡང་གཅིག་གསོན་དང་གྱུབ་ཕོབ་རྡོ་རྗེ་འཛིན། །དུས་དན་
སྒྲིགས་མའི་འགྲོ་ཀུན་རྒྱུན་བརྫོག་ལ། །བན་དེ་རྣམས་ཀྱིས་ཁ་འབར་ཆེན
པོས་བརྫོག །བོན་པོ་རྣམས་ཀྱིས་ཁྲོ་ཆེན་རོལ་པས་བརྫོག །དཔའ་བོ་
མཁའ་འགྲོའི་དགར་གཏོར་ཆེན་པོ་ནི། །བརྒྱ་དང་སོ་ལྔས་འགལ་རྒྱེན་རབ་

ཏུ་བརྣོག །གསུང་རབ་སྙིང་པོ་དམ་པ་བཅུ་གཉིས་ནི། །མང་པོ་ཚོགས
ནས་འདུ་སྤྲ་ཆེན་པོས་བརྣོག །ཚོ་འདིར་བདེ་དང་ཕྱི་མར་བྱང་ཆུབ་འཐོབ། །
ཐེ་ཚོམ་མེད་དོ་སྐལ་ལྡན་རིགས་ཀྱི་བུ། །རྒྱལ་བའི་བཀའ་ལ་བསྐུལ་བ་མི་སྙིང་
པས༔ །མཆོད་པ་ཡིན་པས་བླ་མ་ཡི་དམ་མཉེས། །ཁྲིན་རྣབས་དངོས་གྲུབ
ཆར་ལྟར་འབེབས་པར་འགྱུར། །སྙིན་པ་ཡིན་པས་ལྷ་འདི་གདོན་བགེགས
ཚོམ༔ །སྦྱིན་ལས་འཕྲལ་རྐྱེན་ལན་ཆགས་ཐམས་ཅད་བྱུང་། །ཞི་བ
ཡིན་པས་ཐམས་ཅད་རང་སར་ཞི། །སྙིང་རྗེ་ཡིན་པས་ཐམས་ཅད་བདེ་དང
ལྡན༔ །དྲག་པོ་ཡིན་པས་དགྲ་བགེགས་གཏན་ནས་བརླག །དོན་དམ་ཡིན
པས་རྟོགས་པ་ནང་ནས་འཆར། །ཕར་གྲོལ་ཡིན་པས་རིག་པ་རང་སར
གྲོལ༔ །ཕྱག་ཕྲེང་ཡིན་པས་ཏོ་བོ་ལྷག་གེར་མཐོང་། །གཅེར་བུ་ཡིན་པས
སྒྲིབ་པས་གོས་པ་མེད། །ཐོགས་མེད་ཡིན་པས་རྒྱ་འཕུལ་མཁའ་ལ་འགྲོ། །
རལ་གྲི་ཡིན་པས་རྣོ་བའི་རར་དང་ལྡན། །དགྲ་སྟ་ཡིན་པས་གཅོད་པའི
དབལ་དང་ལྡན། །སྐུ་གྱི་ཡིན་པས་གང་ལ་ཐོགས་པ་མེད། །བགའ་བབ
ཡིན་པས་རྒྱུད་བཞིའི་གསོལ་འདེབས་ཡིན། །དམ་ཚོས་ཡིན་པས་ཕྱག་རྒྱ
ཆེན་པོ་ཡིན། །རྟོགས་པ་ཡིན་པས་ཀུན་རིག་ཀུན་ཕར་རྟོགས། །འབྲས
བུ་ཡིན་པས་ཕྱི་མའི་ས་ལམ་བགྲོད། །བར་ཆད་བརྣོག་པར་ཐེ་ཚོམ་མེད་དོ
བུ༔ །སྙིང་པ་ཡིན་པས་རྐྱེན་ངན་རང་སར་སྟོང་། །རོ་སྙོམས་ཡིན་པས་ལྷས
ངན་རང་སར་གྲོལ། །སྣ་མ་ཡིན་པས་སྟོང་ཉིད་རྟུ་འཕུལ་སྟེབ། །མི་ལྡང
ཡིན་པས་སྟོང་གསུམ་མེ་ཡིས་འཇིག །རྡོ་རྗེ་ཡིན་པས་རང་སེམས་རྡོ་རྗེའི
གྱུར༔ །མཚོན་ཆ་ཡིན་པས་དགྲ་བགེགས་གཏན་ནས་གཅོད། །ཀུན་ཁྱབ

༄༅། །ཡིན་པས་འཁོར་འདས་ཡོངས་ལ་ཁྱབ། །གཅིག་པུ་ཡིན་པས་
སྟོང་གསུམ་རྟ་འཕུལ་སྟེབ། །ལྷ་རུ་ཡིན་པས་ཡི་དག/་སེམས་ལ་ཤར། །
འདི་རུ་ཡིན་པས་སྟོང་པས་སྟོང་པ་གསོད། །འཕོ་བ་ཡིན་པས་དེ་མ་ཐག་ཏུ་
གྲོལ། །དེ་རྣམས་ཐམས་ཅད་རོ་རོར་མ་ཡིན་པར། །མཁན་པོ་གཅིག་གི་
སྟེང་དུ་ཐམས་ཅད་རྫོགས། །དེ་ལྟར་གཅོད་འདི་རྫོགས་པ་ཆེན་པོ་ཡིན། །
རྫོགས་པས་མི་རྫོགས་གང་ཡང་མེད་པ་ཡིན། །སྟོང་ཉིད་བཅོ་བརྒྱད་འདི་རུ་
རྫོགས་པ་ཡིན། །དེ་སྐད་སྒྲོལ་དཔོན་ཉིད་ཀྱི་ཞལ་ནས་གསུངས། །བདག་
ལ་ཡུང་བསྩལ་དེ་རྣམས་ཕྱགས་རྗེ་ཆེ། །བསྐལ་བ་སྙིགས་མའི་སེམས་
ཅན་ཕྱགས་རྗེས་ཟུངས། །སེར་གཟུགས་དཀོར་ཟན་ང་རང་ཕྱགས་རྗེས་
ཟུངས༔ །ཞེས་དེ་ལྟར་གསོལ་བ་བཏབ་པས་སྒྲོལ་དཔོན་ཆེན་པོའི་ཞལ་ནས་
འདི་སྐད་གསུངས། ༈ ཨེ་མ་ཧོཿ ཡང་གཅིག་གསོན་དང་གྲུབ་ཐོབ་
རྗེ་རྗེ་འཛིན། །ཁྱོད་ཉིད་འདི་ནས་ཚོག་མིན་གནས་སུ་གཤེགས། །བདེ་བ་
ཅན་དུ་འོད་དཔག་མེད་མགོན་གྱི། །ཉེ་གནས་མཛད་ནས་ལོ་གསུམ་བར་དུ་
བཞུགས༔ །དེ་ཚེ་ཁྱོད་ཀྱིས་སྐུ་ཚབ་ཕོད་པ་ནི། །ཁྲུམ་རིལ་དག་གི་དབུ་
འདི་སྐུ་ཚབ་ཞིག །རྣམ་པར་རྒྱལ་བའི་ཁང་བཟང་རྒྱན་ལྡན་པ། །དུང་ཁང་
ཡངས་པའི་གཞལ་ཡས་ཕྱི་ནང་ལ། །རྗེན་གྱི་གཙོ་བོ་ཀུན་བཟང་སྣང་མཐའ་
ཡས༔ །དེ་ཡི་མདུན་དུ་བརྒྱ་རྣམ་པར་སྣང་། །ཤར་དུ་རྡོར་སེམས་སྤྲོ་དུ་
རིན་ཆེན་འབྱུང་། །ནུབ་ཏུ་སྣང་མཐའ་བྱང་དུ་དོན་ཡོད་གྲུབ། །བསྐལ་
བཟང་སངས་རྒྱས་སྟོང་དང་གྲུབ་ཆེན་བརྒྱ། །རྒྱལ་བ་རྡོ་རྗེ་འཆང་ཆེན་ལ།
སོགས་པའི། །བརྒྱུད་པའི་བླ་མ་ཆར་སྤྲིན་བཞིན་དུ་འཕྲིགས། །ཕྱག་ལས་

129

རྩིགས་དང་དབུ་མ་ཞི་བྱེད་སོགས། །ཁྱོགས་རིས་མེད་པའི་བཀྱུད་པའི་ཀླུ་
མ་བཞུགས། །བདེ་མཆོག་དགྱེས་རྡོར་གསང་འདུས་གཤིན་དམར་
འཇིགས། །རྒྱུད་སྡེ་བཞི་ཡི་ལྷ་ཚོགས་འཁོར་དང་བཅས། །མ་ལུས་པ་
དང་ལུས་པ་མེད་པའི་ཚོགས། །ཐམས་ཅད་ཆད་བར་བཞུགས་པ་རིས་པ་
ཡིན༔ །གཞན་ཡང་ལྷ་དང་རིང་བསྲེལ་གྲངས་མེད་འབྱོན། །ཁྱོགས་བཅུའི་
སངས་རྒྱས་བྱོང་དང་དབྱེར་མེད་ཡིན། །དེ་ཕྱིར་བྱོང་གྱི་དབུལ་འབྱོན་པར་
འདུག །ཡི་དམ་ལྷ་ཚོགས་བྱོང་དང་དབྱེར་མེད་ཡིན། །ཚོས་སྐྱོང་སྲུང་མ་
བྱོད་དང་འདུ་འབྲལ་མེད། །བྱོང་རང་ཉེན་ལ་དེ་ཕྱིར་འབྱོན་པར་འདུག །
བོད་ཁམས་མི་ལ་ཞལ་ད་དེ་བཞིན་མཛོད། །བྱོད་ཀྱི་དབུལ་ལ་ལྷ་ཚོགས་དེ་
རྣམས་འབྱོན། །མ་འབྱོན་ཚེན་པ་བདུ་ང་ཡིས་བསྐུས། །ཐེ་ཚོམ་མེད་དོ་གྲུབ་
ཐོབ་རྗེ་རྗེ་འཇིང་། །བྱོད་ཀྱི་སེམས་ལ་ཐེ་ཚོམ་གང་ཧར་དེ། །དའི་སྙང་བ་
ཚོས་སྐྱུའི་འོད་ལ་གསལ། །ཐེ་ཚོམ་མ་བྱེད་བོད་ལ་ཞལ་ད་ཞིག །བྱོང་ཀྱི་
རྟེན་གྱིས་བོད་ལ་འགྲོ་དོན་འོང་། །འགྲོ་བ་མི་རིགས་ཤི་གསོན་ཐམས་ཅད་
ཀྱིས༔ །ཚེ་འདིར་སྒྲུབས་མགོན་ཕྱི་མར་བྱང་ཆུབ་ལམ། །སྐྱུར་ད་ཐོབ་པར་
ཐེ་ཚོམ་མེད་དོ་བྱ། །ཁྱག་དང་བསྒོར་བའི་ཐན་ཡོན་ཆེན་པོ་འབྱུང་། །
བསྒོར་གྱངས་ཚད་ནི་བཀྱུ་ཚོ་ཉེར་ལྷུའི། །ཁྱག་གྱངས་ཚད་ནི་བཀྱུ་ཕྱག་ང་
ལྷུའི། །དེ་སྐུད་གསུངས་པས་བདག་གིས་འདི་སྐུད་ཞུས། །བདེ་བ་ཅན་ད་
ལོ་གསུམ་ནི་གནས་ཚེ། །བོད་ལ་མི་རིང་མ་ད་པར་འགྲོ་དོན་ཆག །དི་ཚེ་
བོད་ཀྱི་མི་རྣམས་ཐམས་ཅད་ཀྱིས། །དགོར་གྱིས་བསྐྱབས་ནས་འོང་རྒྱུ་མེད་
དོ་སྐུད། །དེ་སྐུད་ཟེར་ཞིང་སྐུར་པ་མང་ད་འདེབས། །དེ་ལ་དགའ་སྤྲོ

༄༅། །སྣང་བ་མ་མཆིས་ཀྱང་། །འཇིག་རྟེན་མི་ནག་ཀུན་གྱི་ངན་གཏམ་
འདི། །དུས་ངན་སྟོབས་ཀྱིས་མི་བྱེད་འདུག་རྒྱུ་མེད། །སེམས་ཅན་ལས་
ངན་བསགས་པའི་རྒྱུར་འགྲོ་བའི། །ཀྱེ་རུ་ཆོད་ཀྱི་ཕུགས་རྟེས་མཐེན་དུ་
གསོལ༔ །དམ་སྲི་ཕོ་མོའི་བསྟན་པ་ངར་བའི་དུས། །ནམ་མཁའ་ཁྱབ་
མདོག་གནན་སྣར་མཐུག་རིང་ཕར། །བར་སྣང་ཁམས་སུ་གནན་ནན་གྲོག
ལྟར་འཆུབས། །ས་གཞིའི་སྟེང་ནས་གཉན་ལྟོག་མི་ལྟར་འབར། །ཐོག
དང་སེར་བ་གནན་ནད་སྐྱུང་ལྟར་འཆུབས། །ནད་ཀྱི་ན་ཕུན་གདོན་གྱི་བ
ཡུག་འཆུབས། །མ་མོ་འབྲུགས་པས་དུག་གི་སྲུང་ནག་གཡོ། །ནད་མུག
མཚོན་གྱི་བསྐལ་པ་ཐར་བའི་དུས། །མ་མོ་མཁའ་འགྲོའི་ཁྲག་ནད་རིམས
ཡམས་ཀྱིས། །སྲི་འགྲོ་སེམས་ཅན་གྲོ་བར་ནད་ཀྱིས་འཆི། །ས་གཡོ་སྲུང
འཆུབས་རྟོ་ཡི་ཆར་པ་འབབ། །རྒྱུ་ལོག་ཏྲི་སྟོན་ཡུང་སྐྱ་ནད་ནས་རྒྱུག །
ས་ཆད་ཐུག་ཞིག་ཀྲུན་མས་རེ་ཡུང་གང་། །ཁ་ཡུང་ཐམས་ཅད་དགྲ་ཐག
ཁྲམ་གསུམ་ཆུལ། །མི་རྣམས་ཀུན་ལ་གཟེར་ནད་ཕོག་ལྟར་ལྷུང་། །དེ
འདྲའི་དུས་སུ་ཁྱེད་ཀྱི་ཕུགས་རྟེས་ཟུངས། །ཕུགས་རྟེ་མ་ཆུང་གུ་རུ་རིན
པོ་ཆེ། །དུས་ངན་སྟེགས་པའི་འགྲོ་ཀུན་ཕུགས་རྟེས་ཟུངས། །དེ་སྐད
བདག་གིས་གུ་རུ་ཆེན་ལ་ཞུས། །གུ་རུ་པདྨའི་ཞལ་ནས་འདི་སྐད་གསུངས།
༔ ཨེ་མ་ཧོཿ ཡང་གཅིག་གསོན་དང་གྲུབ་ཐོབ་མཐེན་པ་ཅན། །གསལ
སྟོང་སྐྱུ་ལ་སྐྱེའི་སུ་རུའི་མཚན་ཅན་ཁྱོད། །སྟོན་ཆེ་སྐྱེ་བ་མང་པོའི་གོང་རོལ
ཏུ༔ །དགའ་བོའི་སྐྱལ་པ་ལག་ན་རྡོ་རྗེ་འཛིན། །སྐྱལ་པའི་མཐའ་གྱུར་ཆད
མེད་འོད་དང་སྐྱེ། །རྡོ་རྗེ་འཆང་གི་ཉེ་གནས་མཛད་ཅིང་བཞུགས། །དེ

ནས་ཡུས་བོར་རིག་པའི་མཐའ་གྱུར་ནི། །ཤ་ར་ཏ་དང་གྱུ་སྒྲུབ་ལ་སོགས་
ཀྱི། །ཉེ་གནས་མཛད་ནས་ཧྭ་འཁྱལ་ཐོགས་པ་མེད། །དེ་ཕྱིར་ཐོགས་མེད་
ཆོད་ཕྱན་ཞེས་སུ་གྲགས། །དེ་ཉིད་གནས་གྱུར་དག་ལ་ཤེས་རབ་ནི། །གྲུབ་
ཆེན་དེའི་ཡོའི་ཉེ་གནས་མཛད་ནས་བཤགས། །དེ་ཉིད་གནས་གྱུར་འགྲོ་
མགོན་ལོ་ཙྩ་ནི། །ནུ་རོ་ཆེན་པོའི་ཉེ་གནས་མཛད་ཅིང་བཤགས། །དེ་ཉིད་
གནས་གྱུར་རྡོག་ཆེན་ཆོས་རྡོར་ནི། །གྲུབ་ཆེན་མར་པའི་ཉེ་གནས་མཛད་
ནས་བཤགས། །དེ་ཡི་རིག་པའི་མཐའ་གྱུར་རས་ཆུང་པ། །གྲུབ་ཆེན་མི་
ལའི་ཉེ་གནས་མཛད་ནས་བཤགས། །དེ་ཡི་རིག་པའི་མཐའ་གྱུར་གསལ་
སྟོང་པ། །རྣྲ་འོད་གཞོན་ནུའི་ཉེ་གནས་མཛད་ནས་བཤགས། །དེ་ཉིད་
གནས་གྱུར་དག་གི་དབང་ཕྱུག་ཅེས། །རྒྱག་ར་ཡུལ་དུ་བརྗེ་ཏ་རྒྱལ་བྱོན། །
དེ་ཉིད་མི་གནས་སྒྱུ་དང་འདས་འོག་ཏུ། །ཁྲག་སྐྱགས་ཞེས་བུ་འཚོལ་བའི་
བཏུལ་ཞུགས་ཅན། །རང་བྱུང་རྡོ་རྗེའི་ཉེ་གནས་མཛད་ཅིང་བཤགས། །དེ་
ཡི་རིག་པའི་མཐའ་གྱུར་དགེ་སྦྱོང་རྒྱལ། །ཆོས་ཀྱི་དབང་ཕྱུག་བུ་བའི་མཚན་
གསོལ་ནས། །བུ་སྒྱུབ་མང་པོའི་གདུལ་བྱར་འགྲོ་དོན་མཛད། །ཤེམས་
ཅན་མང་པོ་བྱང་རྒྱལ་ལམ་སྦ་དྲངས། །དེ་ཡི་རིག་པའི་མཐའ་གྱུར་ཀཱ་རུ་
སྐྱེས། །དགེ་སྦྱོང་རྒྱལ་འཇོན་ཀཱ་ཆོས་དབང་གྲགས། །འགྲོ་བའི་མགོན་
པོའི་ཉེ་གནས་མཛད་ནས་བཤགས། །སྐུ་གསུངས་ཐུགས་ཀྱི་རྟེན་མཚོག་
མང་དུ་བཞེངས། །སེམས་ཅན་མང་པོ་ཐར་པའི་ལམ་ལ་བཀོད། །དེ་ཡི་
སྒྱལ་པ་སངས་རྒྱས་བསྟན་འཇིན་ཅེས། །སྤྲག་འགོར་སངས་རྒྱས་བསྟན་ལ་
ཆགས་ཕྱིར་མཛད། །དེ་ཉིད་ཕྱི་མར་བསོད་ནམས་བཀྲ་ཤིས་ཞེས། །འགྲོ

132

༄༅། །དོན་ཆོས་ཀྱིས་གདུལ་བྱའི་རེ་བ་བསྐངས། །དེ་རྗེས་མ་ཁབས་
མཆོག་ཤེས་རབ་ཀྱ་མཚོ་ཡིས། །རིས་མེད་རྒྱལ་བསྟན་ཡོངས་ཀྱི་ཞབས་
འབྲིང་མཛད། །སྐྱལ་པའི་མཐའ་གྱུར་གྲུབ་པའི་དབང་ཕྱུག་མཆོག །འགྲོ་
བའི་མགོན་པོ་ཀུན་དགའ་བསོད་ནམས་གྲགས། །ཡང་སྐུལ་དོན་གྲུབ་
མཆན་ཅན་འགྲོ་བ་འདུལ། །སྐྱལ་པའི་ལོད་ཟེར་ཉི་མ་བཀྲ་ཤིས་ཁྲིད། །དང་
དུང་སྐྱེ་བ་བདུན་ལ་འགྲོ་དོན་མཛད། །མ་ཨོངས་འགྲོ་བའི་དོན་ལ་སྤྱོད་པའི་
ཚེ༔ །ཉི་མ་ཤེས་བྱའི་མཚན་ལ་འཕོ་འགྱུར་མེད། །དེ་ནས་མི་གནས་མྱུ་ངན་
འདས་འོག་ཏུ། །གདེར་སྟོན་རྗེ་རྗེའི་མིང་ནི་ཡོངས་སུ་གྲགས། །དེ་དུས་
བཅུལ་ཞུགས་སྐྱལ་བ་དུ་མའི་བདག །ཧ་མཆན་སྐུ་རྒྱུབ་གཡུང་དུང་ཞབས།
སུ་གསལ། །གདེར་ཆོས་དཔག་མེད་དུས་མཐའི་བར་དུ་འདོན། །འགྲོ་དོན་
དཔག་མེད་རྒྱལ་ཁམས་ཅི་མཆིས་ཀྱང་། །གདེར་གྱིས་འགྲོ་དོན་སྐྱེ་བ་མང་
པོར་འབྱུང་། །དེ་ཉིད་མི་གནས་མྱུ་ངན་འདས་འོག་ཏུ། །རྒྱལ་བ་བྱམས་
པའི་ཞབས་དྲུང་གཤེགས་ནས་ཀྱང་། །བྱམས་པ་མི་གཟུགས་འགྲོ་དོན་
མཛད་པའི་དུས། །ཁྱོད་ནི་དགེ་སྐྱོང་ཆ་བྱད་འགྲོ་བ་འདུལ། །བྲམ་ཞེ་
དཔལ་ལྡན་ཞེས་བྱའི་མིང་ཅན་འབྱུང་། །སྐྱར་ཡང་སྐྱེ་བ་བདུན་དུ་འགྲོ་དོན་
མཛད༔ །དེ་ཕྱིར་དུ་མ་རོ་གཅིག་མཛོན་སངས་རྒྱས། །འདི་རྣམས་ང་ཡིས་
ཤེས་པ་མ་ཡིན་ཏེ། །སྒྲིབ་དཔོན་ཆེན་པོ་པདྨ་འབྱུང་གནས་ཀྱིས། །ཡུང་
བསྟན་འདི་རྣམས་ཉམས་སུང་དང་དུ་བྱུང་། །ཞེས་གསུངས་པ་ལ། དཔོན་
པོ་གཉིས་ཀྱིས་ཞུས་པ། ཡུང་བསྟན་དེ་རྣམས་བཀའ་འདྲིན་ཤིན་ཏུ་ཆེ། ང་
ཅིས་ཀྱང་དམ་པ་ཉིད་མི་བཞུགས་ནའང་། དེད་འདིར་ཚོགས་རྣམས་ལ་ཁྲིད་

133

ཀྱིས་སྐྱེ་བ་དྲན་རབས་ཀྱི་ལོ་རྒྱུས་ཤིག་ཞུ་ཞེས་ཞུས་པས། ཡང་བླ་མའི་ཞལ་
ནས་འདི་སྐད་གསུངས། ངས་སྐྱེ་བ་དྲན་རབས་སྟེ་ཡིས་སྐྲ་མི་ནུས། མདོར་
བསྡུས་པ་འདི་རྣམས་དབེན་པོ་སོགས་ཀྱི་ཕྱགས་ལ་ཟིག །བདག་གི་སྐྲི་ལས་
དང་ལྱུང་བསྐུན་ལ་བརྟེན་ནས་བཤད་པར་བྱའོ། །ང་རང་གར་སྐྱེས་པའི་
ཆུལ་བསམ་གྱིས་མི་ཁྱབ་སྟེ། མདོར་བསྡུས་པའི་ལོ་རྒྱུས་དང་སྐྱེ་བ་དྲན་པའི་
རྣམ་ཐར་གཉིས་ལས་གྲུབ་རྟགས་བཤག་པའི་ལོ་རྒྱུས་རྒྱུས་པ་གསལ་སྟོང་གི་
རྣམ་ཐར་ཆེ་བའི་ནང་དུ་གསལ། །བསྡུས་པ་ནི་ཁམས་པ་མི་གསུམ་རྒྱ་གར་
དུ་ཕྱིན་པའི་དུས་ན། ཁོང་རྣམ་པ་གསུམ་དགའས་ལྷ་སྒྲམ་པོའི་གནས་ནང་
ནས་ཚོས་གོས་གཞིག་པ་མཛད་ནས་ནམ་མཁའི་དབྱིངས་སུ་ཐོགས་པ་མེད་
པར་བྱུ་ལྱུར་འཕུར་བ་ལ་བླ་མས་རྒྱུབ་ནས་གཟིགས་པས། གྱུབ་ཐོབ་གཉིས་
པོ་བྱུ་ཚམ་ཡོད་པའི་དུས། གསལ་སྟོང་རྩ་རྱུང་ལ་རང་དབང་ཐོབ་པའི་
རྟགས་སུ་བྱིའུ་ཚམ་ལས་མ་མཐོང་། དེ་ནས་རྒྱ་གར་རྗེ་རྗེ་གནན་དུ་ཕེབས་
པ་ལ། །ཁྱབ་པ་ཆེན་པོའི་རིང་བསྲེལ་རྣམས་རྣམ་པ་གསུམ་ཀྱིས་གྱུབ་རྟགས་
ངང་ནས་ཐོགས་པ་མེད་པར་བྱུངས། དེ་ནས་གནས་ལག་རྣམས་དང་གནས་
ཕྲན་བྱིན་རླབས་ཅན་རྣམས་ཀྱི་གནས་ས་དང་། རྗེ་ཡི་རིལ་བུ་དང་། ཨ་ར་
ར་འབྲས་བུ་ལོ་མ་དང་བཅས་པ་ཚོན་སྒྲུལ་གྱི་སྟེང་པོ་ལ་སོགས་པའི་སྣན་སྣ་
ཐམས་ཅད་མ་ལུས་པ་བོད་དུ་གདན་དྲངས་པའི་ཆོས་ཀ་མཛད་ནས། དེ་
ནས་གསལ་སྟོང་གིས་རྣམ་པ་གཉིས་ལ་ད་ལམ་འི་སྐྱོལ་གསུམ་ལ་བླ་མས་
དུར་ཁྲོད་བསིལ་བ་ཚལ་ནས་བྱམ་ཟིའི་རོ་དང་། ཤིང་ཉ་གྱི་རྟ་དང་ཀོས་
བརྒྱག་ཅན་པའི་རོ་ནག་དང་། དུར་ཁྲོད་ཀྱི་གནས་ས་དང་། གནས་རྗེ

134

༄༅། །དང་། ཨ་རུ་ར་ལོ་མ་སྟེ་སྟུངས་སེ་ཡོད་པ་རྣམས་གདན་དྲོངས་
ཧོག་གསུངས་པ་དེ་རྣམས་ཅི་བྱེད་སྨྲས་པ་ལ། རྣམ་པ་གཉིས་ཀྱིས་འདི་སྐྱང་
ཅེས༔ དའི་སྐོལ་གསུམ་ཀྱིས་རྒྱ་གར་རྡོ་རྗེ་གདན་ནས་བླ་མས་ཅི་དགོས་
གསུངས་པ་དེ་རྣམས་ལོན་ཡོད། དུར་ཁྲོད་བསིལ་བ་ཚལ་ནས་ནི་དེ་ལྟར་
ལོན་མི་འོང་། ཤ་ཟ་མཁའ་འགྲོ་མ་དང་། ཁྲག་འཐུང་མཁའ་འགྲོ་མ་དང་།
ཚོ་ལེན་མཁའ་འགྲོ་མ་དང་། སྲོག་འཕྲོག་མཁའ་འགྲོ་མ་དང་། དབུགས་
སྐྱུད་མཁའ་འགྲོ་མ་རྣམས་ཀྱིས་ཤ་ཁྲག་བར་སྣང་ལ་གཏོར་འགྲོ་བས། དེད་
རང་གསུམ་བོད་དུ་ལོག་འགྲོ་ཞེས་པ་ལ། ཡང་གསལ་སྟོང་གིས་དེ་ལྟར་མི་
འགྲོ་བླ་མའི་གསུང་བསྐུབ་དགོས་ཞེས་སྨྲས། ཡང་རྣམ་པ་གཉིས་ཀྱིས་ཚོ་
འདི་ཕྱི་གཉིས་ཀ་ལ་མི་རྗེད་རྒྱུ་དམ་པའི་ཆོས་ཡིན། དམ་པའི་ལྷ་ཆོས་སྐྱུབ་
པ་ལ་ལུས་དང་སེམས་གཉིས་དགོས། འདི་གཉིས་ཁ་བར་ཁྲལ་འགྲོ་དེས་
འདུག དལ་འབྱོར་མི་ལུས་འདི་རྙེད་དཀའ་བས། དེད་རང་གསུམ་ཕྱིར་
ལོག་འགྲོ། དེད་ཅག་ནི་ལུས་སྣར་བ་འདུག་སྐྱས་པ་ལ། ཡང་གསལ་སྟོང་
གིས་འདི་ལྟར་སྐྱས། བླ་མས་ཅི་གསུང་བསྐུབ་པ་དེ་དམ་ཆོས་ཡིན། དམ་
པའི་ཆོས་ཀྱི་རྒྱུ་བ་བླ་མ་ཡིན། བླ་མའི་བཀའ་དང་འགལ་ན་ཐྲིག་པ་ཡིན།
ང་ནི་བླ་མའི་བཀའ་ལས་འགལ་བར་མི་ནུས་སོ། །ཞེས་སྐྱབས་སོ། །དེ་ནས་
རྣམ་པ་གཉིས་ཀྱིས་འོ་ན་ཁྱོད་རང་ཐེབས་སོང་ན་དགའ་བ་རེད་སྐྱབས་པས།
གསལ་སྟོང་གིས་བླ་མའི་བཀའ་ལས་འདའ་མི་ཌྲ། ང་རེས་ལུས་འདི་མཁའ་
འགྲོ་མས་གཏོར་སོང་ན། ཕྱི་རེས་བླ་མའི་ཕྱགས་རྗེས་ལུས་འདི་བས་དྲག
ཅིག་རྙེད་སྲིད་གསུངས་ནས་ཆོས་གོས་ཀྱིས་གཡོག་པ་མཛད་དེ་དུར་ཁྲོད་

བསིལ་བ་ཆལ་དུ་གཤེགས་པ་ལ། རྣུང་གཏུམ་མོ་དྲག་འདྲེན་གྱི་སྒོ་ནས་ཐེབས་པ་ལ། བོད་རྣམ་པ་གཉིས་ཀྱིས་ཅེད་མོའི་ཆུལ་གྱིས་ད་རེས་སྣུ་ལུས་བོར་ཡང་ཕྱི་ཕྱོབ་ལྟ་མའི་ཕུགས་རྟེས་ནལ་མི་མཐེས་པ་དེ་མེད་ཨེ་འགྲོ་གསུང་སྐྱིང་མཛད་པར་གཟིགས་ནས། གསལ་སྟོང་དེ་ཉིད་རེ་སྐྱལ་ནག་ཕྱུར་དུ་རྒྱག་པ་ལྟ་བུ། སྐྱང་ཆེན་འཕྱད་ལ་ཉལ་བ་ལྟ་བུའི་གྱིབ་ཏུ་ཐེབས་སོང་བ་ལ། བོད་གིས་རྣུང་གཏུམ་མོ་དྲག་འདྲེན་གྱི་སྒོ་བས་ཀྱིས་མཁའ་འགྲོ་མ་རྣམས་ཀྱིས་མེ་ཨི་ཕྱུང་པོ་བསམ་གྱིས་མི་ཁྱབ་པ་ཞིག་ཏུ་མཐོང་ནས་སྣུ་ལུས་དེ་ཉིད་འཛར་འོད་མི་དཔུང་གི་རང་བཞིན་དུ་གྱུབ་པ་ལ་མཁའ་འགྲོ་མ་རྣམས་ཀྱིས་བརྣག་མ་ཐེད་པའོ། །དུར་ཁྲོད་བསིལ་བའི་ཆལ་དུ་ཕམ་ཟེའི་རོ་གཏེར་དུ་ཡོད་པའི་ག་དང་། ཤིན་ཏུ་གྱི་རྟ་ཨ་དུར་རྣམ་པར་རྒྱལ་བ་གསེར་མདོག །བསིལ་བ་ཆལ་གྱི་རོ་ནག་དུ་ཁྲོད་རོ་ཡི་རིལ་བུ། རོ་ལ་ཆོས་སྐྱོང་གི་སྐྱ་རང་བྱིན་མང་པོ། རོ་ལ་གནས་བརྟན་བཅུ་དྲུག་རང་བྱིན་དེ་རྣམས་གདན་དྲངས་ནས༔ སྣ་མའི་མདུན་དུ་ཁྲམ་ཟེ་སྐྱེ་བདུན་གྱི་སྐུ་ག་དང་། ཤིན་ཏུ་གྱི་རྟ་ སོགས་ཡོ་བྱད་ཐམས་ཅད་ཆོགས་འབོར་བཀྲམས་པ་ལྟ་བུ་ཐམས་ཅད་ བསྒྲིགས་ནས་ཁམས་པ་གསལ་སྟོང་དེ་ཉིད་ཆོས་གོས་ཀྱིས་དབུ་གཏུམས་དེ་ བཞུགས་པ་ལ། དེ་ནས་རྒྱུ་ཆོད་གསུམ་གྱི་སྟེང་ནས་རྣམ་པ་གཉིས་ཐེབས་ པས༔ རྣམ་པ་གཉིས་ཀྱིས་འདི་ད་རེས་དུར་ཁྲོད་བསིལ་བ་ཆལ་དུ་ཐབལ་ ཡང་འདིར་ཐེབས་འདུག །ཨོ་སྒྲོལ་གཉིས་ལམ་ལ་ནི་མ་འགྲོར་ཀྱང་འདི་ ལ་བདེན་པ་ནི་ཡོད། ཨོ་སྒྲོལ་གཉིས་ནི་བདེན་མེད་འདུ་བས། འདི་ཅི་ ཡིན་པར་འདུག་གསུངས་ཞལ་ཆ་ཆ་ཞིག་བྱུང་ནས་ཁྲོ་ཆིག་འཆལ་བ་འགགའ

༄༅། །གསུང་བ་ལ། བླ་མའི་ཞལ་ནས་འདི་སྐད་གསུངས། སྟོད་
དང་ཕྱུར་པའི་གྲུབ་ཐོབ་གཉིས་པོ་གོ་བ་མ་ལོག་པར་གསོན་དང་། དེ་ཡང་
གསལ་སྟོང་སྐོམ་དུ་འདི་རྟོ་རྗེ་འཆང་གི་དུས་སུ་ཐོབ་གས་མེད་འོད་ལྡན། དུ
ལོའི་དུས་སུ་དག་པ་ཤེས་རབ། ནུ་རོའི་དུས་ན་འགྲོ་མགོན་ལོ་ཙྪ། མར་
པའི་དུས་སུ་རྟོག་སྟོན་ཆོས་རྟོར། མི་ལའི་དུས་སུ་རས་ཆུང་རྡོར་གྲགས།
ངའི་དུས་སུ་ཁམས་པ་གསལ་སྟོང་། དེ་ཡང་གྲུབ་ཐོབ་ཆེན་པོ་ཐོགས་མེད་
འོད་ལྡན་དེ་ཉིད་རྒྱ་གར་ནས་གྲུབ་ཆེན་བཀྱུད་ཅུས་གྲུབ་ཐགས་བཞག་པའི་
དུས། ནམ་མཁའ་ལ་བྱ་ལྟར་འཕུར། རྒྱལ་ཏུ་ལྟར་འགྲོ་བ། རི་རབ་ལ་
ཟང་ཐལ་དུ་འགྲོ་བ། ཕྱག་རྒྱ་དང་ལྷན་ཅིག་ཏུ་ནམ་མཁའ་ལ་གཤེགས་པ་
དང་། གྲུབ་ཐགས་མཉམ་པའི་ནང་ནས་འདི་རྗེ་རྗེའི་བྲག་རི་ལ་ཟང་ཐལ་དུ་
ཐོགས་པ་མེད་པར་འགྲོ་ནུས་པ་ཡིན་ནོ། །གྲུབ་ཐགས་ཐོགས་པ་མེད་པ་
དེའི་དོན་གྱིས་རྒྱ་གར་པས་ཐོགས་མེད་འོད་ལྡན། ཆད་ཡ་མེད་པས་ཆད་
མེད་འོད་ལྡན། གྲུབ་ཐོབ་འདི་ལ་མཚན་གཉིས་ཐོགས་གསུངས། ཡང་
གྲུབ་ཐོབ་རྣམ་གཉིས་ཀྱིས་རྗེ་རྗེའི་བྲག་ལ་ཐོགས་མེད་ཙེ་ལྟར་ལགས་ཞུས་
པས། རྒྱ་གར་འཕགས་པའི་ཡུལ་དུ་གྲུབ་ཐོབ་ཀུ་ཀུ་རི་པ་དང་གྲུབ་ཐགས་
བཞག་པའི་དུས་སུ་གྲུབ་ཐོབ་འདི་ཉིད་ཕྱག་རྒྱ་དང་ལྷན་ཅིག་ཏུ་བྲག་རི་རྗེ་མོ་
དགུང་དུ་མཉམ་པ་ཞིག་ཡོད་པའི་རྗེ་མོ་ནས་རྩ་བར་ཟང་ཐལ་དུ་ཕྱུད། ཡང་
རྩ་བ་ནས་རྩེ་མོར་ཕྱུད། ཡང་བྲག་རི་དེའི་འདམ་ཐབ་དུ་མདའ་ལྟར་ཕྱུད།
དེ་འདྲ་བའི་གྲུབ་ཐགས་ལ་ཆད་ལ་མེད་པར་བྱུང་བས། རྒྱ་གར་པས་ཆད་
མེད་འོད་ལྡན་ཞེས་གྲགས་སོ། །དེའི་སྐྱེས་མཐའ་འགྱུར་བ་མེད་པ་ཡིན
137

ཅེས་གསུངས་པ་ལ། ཡང་རྣམ་པ་གཉིས་ཀྱིས་འོད་ཟུན་ཟེར་བ་ཅི་ལྟར་
ལགས་ཞུས་པས། བླ་མའི་ཞལ་ནས་འོད་ཟུན་ཟེར་བ་བསྐྱེ་བ་མང་པོ་བརྒྱུད་
པའི་བར་སྐྱབས་ལ། ཧ་བདུན་དབང་པོའི་ཚ་ཟེར་འོད་ཀྱིས་སྐྱིང་བཞི་ཀུན་
ལ་ཁྱབ་པའི་མཚན་ཡོངས་སུ་གྲགས་པའོ། །དེ་ནས་རྣམ་པ་གཉིས་ཐེ་ཚོམ་
དང་བྲལ་ནས། དཔོན་སློབ་ཐམས་ཅད་ཀྱིས་ཚོགས་འབོར་རྒྱ་ཆེན་པོ་
མཛད་ཏཿ དེ་རྣམས་གྲུབ་ཏུགས་བཞག་པའི་ལོ་རྒྱུས་བསྡུས་པའོ། །དསྐྱེ་བ་
དུན་པའི་ལོ་རྒྱུས་རྒྱས་པར་བཤད་ན་ལྗེས་སླ་མི་ནུས་པས། མདོར་བསྡུས་
ཙམ་ཞིག་བཤད་ན་ནི། །ཁམས་པ་མི་གསུམ་གྱི་དུས་སུ་གསལ་སྟོང་སྒོམ་དྲ་
དེའི་སྐྱལ་པ་ནི་རྗེ་རང་བྱུང་རྡོ་རྗེའི་དུས་རྒྱ་གར་ཡུལ་དུ་ཧར་སྐྱོ་ཞུང་བའི་རྒྱལ་
པོ་ཞིག་ལ་སྲས་གསུམ་ཡོད་པའི་ཐ་ཆུང་། མིང་བཀྲི་ཏ་དགའ་གི་དབང་ཕྱུག
ཅེས་པའི་ལོ་རྒྱུས་མདོ་རྒྱུད་ཀུན་ནས་གསལ་བ་དེ་ཡིན། དེའི་སྐྱལ་པ་རྟོགས་
ལྡན་ཁག་སྐྱུགས་ཞེས་བྱ་བའི་མིང་ཡོངས་སུ་གྲགས་པ་དེ་ཉིད་ཕྱགས་མཐོ་
དམན་གྱི་ཆུལ་བསྟན་ནས་གྲུབ་ཏགས་རྟ་འཕུལ་ཕོགས་པ་མེད་པའི་སློ་ནས་
བརྗེས་སྐྱེས་ཀྱི་ལྭ་འཇེའི་རིགས་ཐམས་ཅད་དབང་དུ་བསྡུས། ཁྱད་པར་
སོག་ལྷགས་ཟམ་ཁའི་དགེ་བསྙེན་གདུག་པའི་སེམས་དང་ལྡན་པ་ཏྲ་མཿའི་ང་
རོས་སྲིད་པ་གསུམ་ཡང་འགོངས་ཤིང་གཡོ་ནུས་པའི་དགེ་བསྙེན་དྲག་རྩལ་
ཅན་དེ་ཡང་མཛོན་སྤྱམ་བླ་མའི་མདུན་དུ་ཁས་ལེན་དམ་བཅའ་ཕུལ་ལ་ཁྲིད
འོང་ནུས་པ་དེ་ལྟར་དང་། དེའི་སྐྱལ་པ་གཙང་གི་ནམ་པོ་ལྱང་དུ་དགེ་སློང
ཚོས་ཀྱི་དབང་ཕྱུག་བྱ་བའི་མཚན་གསོལ་ནས་རང་གཞན་ལ་ཕན་པའི་གདུལ་
བྱར་གྱུར་པའི་བུ་སློབ་མང་པོར་བྱོན། དེའི་སྐྱལ་པ་གཀྲུར་སྐྱེས་ནས་གཀྲུའི

138

༄༅། །གདན་ས་ཆེན་པོ་ལོ་དགུ་བཟུང་ནས་སྐུ་གསུང་ཐུགས་ཀྱི་རྟེན་
མཆོག་མང་དུ་བཞེངས་པ་དང་། སེམས་ཅན་གྱི་དོན་དཔག་ཏུ་མེད་པར་
མཛད། དེའི་སྐྱལ་པ་སྐ་སྨུག་འགོར་སྐྱེས་ནས་སེམས་ཅན་ལ་ཕན་ཕྱིར་ལོ་
བཅུ་གསུམ་དུ་རངས་རྒྱས་བསྟན་པའི་ཕྱག་ཕྱིར་བྱས། དེའི་སྐྱལ་པ་པཱ་སར་
སྐྱེས་ནས་མིང་དགེ་སྦྱོང་བསོད་ནམས་བཀྲ་ཤིས་བུ་བའི་མཆན་གསོལ་ཏེ་
དགེ་འདུན་རྣམས་ལ་ཆོས་ཀྱི་འཁོར་ལོ་རྒྱ་ཆེན་པོ་བསྐོར་ནས་འགྲོ་དོན་
དཔག་ཏུ་མེད་པ་མཛད། དེའི་སྐྱལ་པ་མཁས་མཆོག་ཤེས་རབ་རྒྱ་མཚོ་ཞེས་
བུ་བའི་མཆན་གྲགས་པས་རྒྱ་མཚོའི་གོས་ཅན་གྱིས་བསྟན་པའི་ཕྱག་ཕྱིར་
མཛད། དེའི་སྐྱལ་པ་ལེགས་གཡག་འགོར་སྐྱེས། སྐྱེས་དན་ཀུན་དགའ་
བསོད་རྣམས་བུ་བའི་མཆན་གསོལ་ཏེ། སྐུ་དང་སྐུར་རོང་གསུམ་གྱི་བླ་མ་
མཛད་ནས་འགྲོ་བའི་དོན་དཔག་མེད་མཛད། གཞན་ཡང་ཁྱད་པར་
འཕགས་པའི་ཕྱིར་འགྲོ་རྒྱལ་ལན་བདུན་འཕུར། གྲོ་ཡུལ་ཕང་འགོ་ནས་ང་
རང་གསལ་སྟོང་སྒོམ་པོའི་སྐྱེས་མཐའ་ཡིན་ཟེར་རོ་ལ་ཞབས་རྗེས་བདུན་
བཞག །ལམ་འདྲེ་བཤའ་སྟེབ་དམ་ལ་བདགས། ཕྱག་མཁར་ཕུག
ལ་བཅུགས། གཞན་ཡང་ར་རེན་བཞགས་པའི་དུས་སུ་སྐྱབ་རྒྱ་འདོན་པ་
ལ་སོགས་པའི་གྲུབ་རྟགས་དོ་མཆར་ཅན་བསམ་གྱིས་མི་ཁྱབ་པ་མང་པོ་
བཞག །དེ་ཡིད་ཞིང་ཁམས་སུ་བྱོན་ས་མཛོད་ཉག་ཡིན། དེའི་སྐྱལ་པ་སྐྱེ་
དན་བགྲ་ཤིས་དོན་འགྲུབ་ཡིན། དེའི་སྐྱལ་པ་ཉི་མ་བགྲ་ཤེས་ང་ཡིན
གསུངས་པས། དབོན་པོ་གཉིས་ཀྱིས་ཞུས་པ། རྣམ་ཐར་དེ་རྣམས་
གསུངས་པ་བཀའ་དྲིན་ཆེ། ང་ཡང་སྐྱལ་པའི་སྐུ་ཡང་ཡང་འབྱོན་པར་ཞུ

139

ཞེས་ཞུས་པས། སྐྱེ་བ་ལེན་པ་ལ་དགའ་བ་རྒྱུ་མི་འདུག །ང་རང་བསམ་པ་ལ་བདེ་བ་ཅན་དུ་དགའ་བར་འདུག །བོད་འདིར་འོངས་ཀྱང་ཡུལ་ཁམས་ཐམས་ཅད་དམག་གིས་གང་། ནད་དང་མུ་གེ་མཚོན་གྱི་བསྐལ་པ་ཡང་དར་བས་འོངས་འཚོར་གསུངས། ཡང་དབོན་པོ་གཉིས་ཀྱིས་ཁྱོད་བོད་ཆེན་གྱི་ལྡོངས་འདིར་སྟོར་སྐྱུད་བར་གསུམ་གང་ལ་ཡང་བྱོན་པའི་དུས་སུ་བདག་སོགས་ཡོན་བདག་པོ་མོ་ཚོས་སྐྱོར་ཞུགས་པ་ཐམས་ཅད་དང་པ་མེད་མཁན་མེད་པས་ཕྱི་རབས་རྣམས་ལ་ཕྱག་དང་མཆོད་པ་བསྐོར་བའི་རྟེན་དུ་ཅིག་ཅུར་མ་འབྱོན་གྱི་བར་དུ་དབུ་ཕྱོད་འཇོག་པར་ཞུ་ཞེས་ཞུས་པས། བླ་མས་དབུ་ལ་ཕྱག་གིས་བྱུགས་ནས། འོ་ན་འདི་ལྟར་འབྱོན་སྲིད་པས་ཁྱེད་རང་རྣམས་ཀྱིས་བསྐུན་པ་དང་སེམས་ཅན་ལ་གང་ཕན་གྱིས། ང་ཡི་རྟེན་ལ་ལྟ་དང་རིང་བཞེལ་འདི་ལྟར་འབྱུང་། སྨིན་མཚམས་སུ་མཛོད་སྤྲུ་མཚོན་པའི་ཕྱིར་མེ་ཏོག་པདྨ་དཀར་པོ་འདབ་མ་བརྒྱུད་པ། བསྐྱེད་རིམ་ལ་བརྟན་པ་ཐོབ་པའི་རྟགས་སུ་དཔྱལ་བ་གཡས་སུ་འཕགས་པ་སྤྱན་རས་གཟིགས། དཔྲལ་བ་གཡོན་དུ་མ་གཅིག་ལབ་སྒྲི་སྒྲོལ་མ་ལ་རིགས་བཞི་མཁའ་འགྲོའི་དཀྱིལ་འཁོར་དང་བཅས་པ་འབྱོན། མཚོག་གསང་གི་སྟེང་དུ་སྟོན་པའི་གཙོ་བོ་ཤཱཀྱ་ཐུབ་པ། དེ་ནས་རྒྱལ་བ་རྡོ་རྗེ་འཆང་གི་རྣམ་འཕྲུལ་རྗེ་ས་ར་ཧ་ཕྱག་མཚན་མདའ་དང་བཅས་པ་འབྱུན། སངས་རྒྱས་བསྟན་པའི་ཞིང་སྐྱོང་བའི་ཕྱིར་ཞིང་སྐྱོང་ཡབ་ཡུམ། ཀུན་ཏུ་བཟང་པོའི་རྣམ་འཕྲུལ་ཆོས་ཀྱི་སྟོན་མ་མཆེད་ལྔ་འབོར་ཤ་ཟ་དམར་ནག་དང་བཅས་པ། རྣ་ལྷག་གཡོན་དུ་རྗེ་བཙུན་མི་ལ་རས་པ་དེ་ཉིད་ཤིན་ཏུ་གྱི་ད་ལ་སྣ་རྒྱབ་གཏད་ནས་མགྱར་གསུང་པའི་ཚུལ་དུ

༄༅། །འབྱུན། རྣ་ལྷག་གཡས་སུ་མ་རྒྱུད་ཡོངས་ཀྱི་གཙོ་མོ་རྡོ་རྗེ་ཕག་
མོ་ལྷ་ལྷ་དཀྱིལ་འཁོར་དང་བཅས་པ་འབྱུན། ལྷག་ཁྲུང་གཡོན་དུ་དཔལ་
འཁོར་ལོ་བདེ་མཆོག་གི་དཀྱིལ་འཁོར་ཡོངས་སུ་རྫོགས་པ་འབྱུན། ལྷག་
པའི་བདུད་སྐྲོ་རུ་ཡེ་ཤེས་ཀྱི་ཁྱུང་ཁྲ་འབྱུན། ཚོས་ཕྱག་རྒྱ་ཆེན་པོ་ལ་མངའ་
བརྙེས། སྟོང་པ་ཉིད་ཀྱི་དོན་རྟོགས་པའི་དགའས་སུ་ལྷག་ཁྲུང་གཡས་སུ་ཚོས་
སྐུ་སྐྱེ་བ་མེད་པའི་ཨྃ་དཀར་པོ་འབྱར་དོད་དུ་འབྱུན། གཞན་ཡང་རྡོ་རྗེ་
སེམས་དཔའ་གསང་བ་འདུས་པ་དགྱིས་པ་རྡོ་རྗེ་ལ་སོགས་པའི་དཀྱིལ་
འཁོར་དང་། བེར་ནག་ཅན་མ་མགོན་དབྱེར་མེད། དམ་ཅན་རྡོ་རྗེ་ལེགས་
པ། ཡང་རིང་བཞིལ་མེ་ཤེལ་མདོག་དང་རྒྱ་ཤེལ་མདོག །བར་མཆམས་
སུ་ཐིག་ལེ་དཀར་དམར་དང་འཛའ་འོད་ཟེར་ཁ་དོག་སྣ་ལྔ་དང་ལྷུན་པའི་ནང་
དུ་སྐུ་གསུགས་དང་རིང་བཞིལ་དཔག་ཏུ་མེད་པ་ཅིས་གྱང་ལས་འདས་པ་
སྟིན་ཕྱུང་འཕྲིགས་པ་ལྟར་ཁྱུ་ཡི་ལེར་བཞུགས། དེ་རྣམས་ཕྱི་རུ་བཞུགས་
པའི་ལྷ་ཚོགས་སོ། །དེ་ནས་ནང་དུ་བཞུགས་པའི་ལྷ་ཚོགས་འདི་ལྷ་སྟེ།
ཧེན་གྱི་གཙོ་བོ་ཀུན་བཟང་སྦྱང་མཐའ། དེའི་འཁོར་དུ་རིགས་ལྔའི་སངས་
རྒྱས་བཀའ་བཞང་སངས་རྒྱས་སྟོང་རྩ་གཉིས། རྒྱ་གར་གྲུབ་ཆེན་བརྒྱད་ཅུ་
ཉེ་སྲས་བརྒྱད། འཕགས་པའི་གནས་བརྟན་བཅུ་དྲུག །རྒྱལ་བ་རྡོ་རྗེ་
འཆང་ལ་སོགས་པའི་ཕྱག་ཆེན་ལམ་འབྲས་རྟོགས་པ་ཆེན་པོ་ལྷ་ལྷན་དབུ་མ
ཉི་བྱེད་སོགས་ཕྱོགས་རིས་མེད་པའི་བརྒྱུད་པའི་བླ་མ་ཆར་སྤྲིན་འཕྲིགས་པ
བཞིན་དུ་བཞུགས། དེ་ནས་རྒྱུད་སྟེ་བཞི་དང་། ཐེག་པ་རིམ་དགུའི་ལྷ
ཚོགས་རྣམས་དང་། ཚོས་སྐྱོང་བོར་ལྔ། མཆོར་ན་བསྐལ་པ་བཟང་པོའི

སངས་རྒྱས་སྟོང་རྩ་གཉིས་ཀྱི་བསྟན་པ་སྲུང་བའི་ཆོས་སྐྱོང་སྲུང་མའི་རིགས་
དྲག་རྩལ་རྫས་འཇིགས་གཏུམ་པའི་ཆ་བྱད་ཅན་གདུག་པའི་སེམས་དང་ལྡན་
པའི་ཚོགས་དཔག་ཏུ་མེད་པ་རྣམས་ཀྱིས་བསྟན་པ་སྲུང་བའི་ཆུལ་དུ་བཞུགས་
པས༑ སྣ་མ་གང་ཟག་དགེ་བའི་བཤེས་གཉེན་དང་། ཚོས་པ་བཟང་པོའི་
རིགས་ལ་སོགས་པའི་བློ་ཚོས་དང་མཐུན་པའི་ཡོན་བདག་དམ་ཚིག་ལ་
མངོན་ལྔོག་དང་སེལ་མ་སོང་བའི་རིགས་མ་གཏོགས། དམ་ཚིག་ལ་སེལ་
སོང་བ་དང་། སྲིག་ཆེན་ལོག་ལྟ་ཅན་དམ་ཉམས་མ་རུངས་པའི་རིགས་
རྣམས་ཀྱིས་དུང་ཁང་འོག་ནས་མཐའ་ལ་མི་རུང་ཞིང་། མཐའ་ན་ཚོས་སྐྱོང་
སྲུང་མ་རྣམས་ཀྱིས་ཕྱག་དོག་བྱེད་ནས་མ་རུངས་པའི་རིགས་ལ་གཟེར་རྗུག་
རྒྱབ་ཉེན་ཡོད་པས་མཇལ་མི་རུང་ཞེས་གསུངས་སོ། །དབོན་པོ་གཉིས་ཀྱིས་
ལྷ་དེ་ལྷ་བྲུར་ཕྱིན་ནའང་། དེ་རྣམས་ཕྱིས་སྣ་ཡིན་ན་ཅི་ཚམ་བཞུགས་ཞུས་
པས༑ དཀྱིལ་རང་རྣམས་ཀྱིས་ལྷ་ཁང་ག་བ་བཞི་ཡི་ཆ་ཚོད་ཡིན་སྐོས། དེ་
ཡན་མ་སྨྲ་མ་གཏོགས་སེར་གསུགས་ང་རྒྱལ་ཅན་དང་སྐྱེ་བོ་དྲེགས་པ་གདུག་
སེམས་ཅན་དང་། རང་སེམས་མ་དག་པའི་ལས་ངན་བློ་མ་རིག་པའི་གདུང་
སེམས་ཅན་རྣམས་ཀྱིས་ལོག་པར་བལྟ་བའི་གཏུམ་སྟྭ་ཡོང་དོགས་ཡོད། ད་
ནས་བཟུང་སྟེ་དུས་ནི་དེ་དན་འགྲོ། མི་རྣམས་ནི་སྲིག་སེམས་དེ་ཆེར་འོང་།
སྲིག་པ་གསོག་པའི་མི་དགེའི་ལས་ནི་དེ་སྐྱབ་འོང་། ལྷ་བླ་མས་ཚོས་འཁོར་
བསྐོར་བའི་དུས། དེ་ལ་མི་དགེའི་ལོག་པར་བལྟ་ཞིང་བསྐུར་པ་འདེབས་པ་
དེ་འདྲ་ནི་ལོ་རེ་སོང་ཡང་རྗེ་བྱུ་ཡིན། མ་རུངས་པའི་རིགས་རྣམས་ཀྱིས་ཀྱང་
པ་ཕོར་གང་མལ་ལ་ལྷ་དེ་དག་ཚམ་ག་ལ་ཡོང་ཟེར་འོང་། དེས་ན་བྱེད་རང་

142

༄༅། །རྩམས་ཀྱིས་གནན་ལ་སྨྲ་ཁང་ཀ་བ་བཞི་ཡན་མ་སྟྲ་དང་ལེགས།
ང་ཡི་དུང་ཁང་ནང་ལ་སྨྲ་ཁང་ཀ་བ་བརྒྱུད་པའི་མལ་གྱི་སྨྲ་འབྲོན་པར་འདུག
ཅེས་གསུངས་སོ། །ཡང་དབོན་པོ་གཉིས་ཀྱིས་ཞུས་པ། ལགས་སྨྲ་ཆེའི
ཆད་བྱས་ན་རྗེ་ཙམ་ལགས་དང་། བྱིན་རྣབས་ཙེ་ཙམ་ཡོད། ཕྱག་དང་
བསྐོར་བའི་ཆད་ལ་ཕན་ཡོན་ཅི་ལྟར་བཞིངས། སྐུ་དང་བྱོན་སྐུ་གཉིས་ལ
ཕྱགས་རྗེ་ཆེ་ཆུང་རྗེ་ལྟར་ལགས། སྨྲ་དེ་རྩམས་དུས་གཅིག་ལ་འབྲོན་ནས
རིམ་བཞིན་འབྲོན། སྨྲ་ཆེ་ཆུང་ཆད་ཙེ་ཙམ་བཤགས་ཞེས་ཞུས་པས། བླ
མས་ང་ཡི་དུང་ཁང་གི་སྨྲ་རྣབས་ཆེན་པོ་བྱས་ན་ཀ་བ་བརྒྱ་ཡི་མལ་ཡོང་སྲིད།
འདི་མཇལ་བའི་ཕན་ཡོན་ཀྱང་བོད་དོ་རྗེ་གནན་དང་གཉིས་སུ་མེད།
སེམས་བསྐྱེད་པའི་ཕྱག་ལ་བརྒྱ་ཕྱག་ང་ལྟ་རེ། བསྐོར་བ་བརྒྱ་ཕྱག་ཉེར
ལྟའི་བར་དུ་བསྐོར་ན་དེ་དག་དུང་གི་ཆང་ཡོང། ཕྱགས་རྗེའི་བཞེངས་སྐུ་ཡི
མ་གསུམ་ལས་རང་བྱོན་གཅིག་དོ་མཆར་ཆེ་བར་འདུག །སྨྲ་ཆེ་བའི་ཆད
ཡུངས་ཀར་ཙམ། རྒྱང་བ་དྲུལ་ཕྱན་ཙམ་དུ་འབྲོན་ཡོང་། གཟུང་འཛིན་གྱི
སྨྲ་ནི་དབུ་སྐྲ་ཏག་མ་རེ་རེའི་རྒྱུད་ཀྱི་ནང་དུ་འབྲོན། རྟེན་མཆོག་འགྲོ་དོན
རྒྱས་བཞིན་སྨྲ་ཐམས་ཅད་འབྲོན། །ཞེས་གསུངས་པས། དེ་རྩམས
གསུངས་པ་བཀའ་དྲིན་དང་དོ་མཆར་ཆེའོ། །ད་བྱོན་གྱི་སྐུལ་སྐུ་ཡང་ནས
ཡང་དུ་མ་བྱོན་ན། འགྲོ་བའི་དོན་དཔག་ཏུ་མེད་པ་ཆག་འགྲོ་བར་འདུག
པས་ཁམས་གསུམ་སེམས་ཅན་བསད་ལས་སྡིག་ཆེའོ། །ཞེས་ཞུས་པས།
བླ་མའི་ཕྱགས་ཏ་ལས། ཨ་ཡ་འདོ། བརྗོད་སྟོབས་དང་སྟེང་སྟོབས་ཆེན་པོ
ཡ་འདོ་གསུངས་པས་ཁོང་གཉིས་ཀྱང་ཞིན་ཏུ་སྐྱག །བླ་མའི་ཞལ་ནས་འདི

སྐད་གསུངས། །ངའི་མི་གནས་མྱུ་དྲན་འདས་ལོག་ཏུ། །སྒྱུལ་པའི་སྐུ་ནི་
རིམ་བཞིན་འབྱོན་ནས་འོང་། །མི་འོང་བསམས་ཀྱང་སེམས་ཅན་སྲིག་ལ་
སྐྱག །དེ་བས་ང་རང་བདེ་བ་ཅན་ན་དགའ། །སངས་རྒྱས་འོད་དཔག་མེད་
པའི་དྲུང་དུ་ནི། །ཉེ་གནས་བྱེད་ནས་སངས་རྒྱས་ཞལ་མཇལ་བས། །བདེ་
སྐྱིད་འདུག་སྟེ་སེམས་ཅན་སྲིག་ལ་སྐྱག །དེ་ཕྱིར་ང་ཡིས་བོད་ལ་འགྱོ་དོན་
བྱེད། །རྒྱ་ཆེ་རྒྱུན་མི་འཁད་པའི་སྒྱུལ་སྒྱུ་འབྱོན། །ང་ཡི་མིང་ནི་ཉི་མ་བཀྲ་
ཤིས་ཟེར། །སྒྱུལ་སྒྱུས་འགྱོ་བའི་དོན་ལ་དགོངས་པའི་ཚེ། །ཉི་མ་ཞེས་
བྱའི་མཚན་ལ་འཕོ་འགྱུར་མེད། །ང་ཡི་དབུ་ཕྱོད་གནས་འདིར་བཞག་པ་
ཡིན། །ང་ཡི་ཆེ་བས་ཆེན་དང་ཉི་ཆེབས་ཆུང་གི། །ཞབས་ཀྱི་རྗེས་ནི་སྒྱུང་
རུའི་འོག་ཏུ་གསལ། །ང་ཡི་དབུ་ཕྱོད་བཞག་པའི་དུས་འདི་ནས། །སྒྱུལ་
པའི་སྐུ་ནི་ན་རིམ་འདས་པའི་སྐབས། །ལོ་གཉས་ཉི་ཤུའི་ཡང་ཕྱོག་འདས་ན་
ཡང་། །ཆེ་ཆུང་མེད་པའི་དབུ་ཕྱོད་དུམ་རེ་འཇོག །དེ་ནི་ཕྱགས་རྟེན་གཙོ་
བོར་བྱས་ན་ལེགས། །ང་ཡི་སྒྱུལ་པ་སྒུ་གསུངས་ཕྱགས་ཀྱང་འབྱོན། །དེ་
དུས་སུམ་ཅུ་ཁ་རལ་ཡང་ཉེའི་ཏྲགས། །འཇིག་རྟེན་མི་ནག་ཕོ་མོ་ཐམས་ཅད་
ཀྱིས། །འདི་ཡིན་འདི་མིན་ནེ་ཚོའི་སྐད་དང་འདྲ། །ཐམས་ཅད་མ་འགགས་
སྣང་ལོ་ཅན་གྱི་གནས། །རྗེ་རྗེ་འཛིན་པའི་ཕྱགས་ཀྱི་སྒྱོང་དུ་གཅིག །དེ་
ཕྱིར་ངའི་རས་རྒྱུད་རྗེ་རྗེར་བྱགས། །ལན་རེར་སྒྱུན་རས་གཟིགས་དབང་
བྱགས། །ལན་རེར་ཕྱག་ན་རྗེ་རྗེར་བྱགས། །ལན་རེར་དྲེགས་པ་ཀུན་
འདུལ་བྱགས། །ལན་རེར་རྗེ་རྗེའི་བུ་ཆུང་བྱགས། །ལན་རེར་དྲག་སྲུགས།
སྲོང་པོ་ཡིན། །ལན་རེར་གཅུམ་པོ་གཟའ་རམ་ཡིན། །ལན་རེར་བླ་མ

༄༅། །གཉེན་རས་ཡིན། །ལེན་རེར་གུ་སྐུ་ཆེན་པོ་ཡིན། །ཐམས་ཅད་
རྡོ་རྗེའི་སྐྱོང་དུ་གཅིག །ཅེས་གསུངས་པ་ལས། ཁོང་གི་བུ་ཆེན་གྱི་གྲལ་
ནས་ཡོན་ཏན་ཆེན་པོ་བསྒྲུབས་པ་བྱེར་དབྱངས་སོགས་རིག་པའི་གནས་ལ་
མཁས་ཤིང་ཐོགས་པ་མེད་པ། བདག་བསྟོད་གཞན་ལ་སྨོད་པ། བླ་མ་གང་
ཟག་དགེ་བའི་བཤེས་གཉེན་ལ་དད་པ་མེད་པ། གཞན་གྱི་ཚོས་ཡུས་ལ་
ཕྱོགས་རིས་དང་ང་རྒྱལ་གྱི་རང་བཞིན་དུ་འདུག་པས་གཏམ་འཆལ་བ་སྨྲས་
པ༔ དེ་ནི་སྟོང་གཏམ་ཡིན་པར་འདུག །སྐྱེ་བ་དེ་ཚམ་ག་ལ་དེན་སྨྲས་པ་ལ།
དེ་མ་ཐག་ཏུ་བླ་མས་མཐིན་ནས། ཁོང་གིས་ཚོད་གསལ་ཕྱག་རྒྱ་ཆེན་པོ་དང་
རྫོགས་པ་ཆེན་པོའི་དང་ནས་དུས་གསུམ་གྱི་སྐྱེ་བ་དྲན་པ་འདི། ཡང་དག
པའི་ཚོས་ཀྱི་ཕྱགས་རྗེ་ཡིན། ཏིང་ངེ་འཛིན་གྱི་སྟོབས་ལས་རང་བྱུང་དུ་ཤར་
བ་ཡིན་ཏེས་གྱང་། སེམས་ཅན་ལས་ཟད། སངས་རྒྱས་མཐུ་རྟགས།
ལས་དན་མ་རུངས་པའི་སེམས་ཅན་རྣམས་ལ་ལོག་པར་ལྟ་བའི་སྐྱོན་འདི་ལྷ་
བུ་ཞུགས་འདུག་དགོངས་ནས། ཁོ་རང་ལ་སྙིང་རྗེ་ཆེན་པོ་སྐྱེས་ཏེ་ཕྱགས་
དགོངས་ཆེན་པོ་མཛད་པ་ལ། ཁར་ཞིན་ནས་སེར་གཟུགས་ང་རྒྱལ་ཅན་
དང་༔ སྐྱེ་པོ་རིགས་པ་གདགས་སེམས་ཅན་གྱི་རིགས་རྣམས་ཀྱིས་ལོག
པར་ལྟ་བའི་གཏམ་སྐྱུ་ཞོང་ཟེར་བ་དེ་ཁོས་གོ་ཨེ་ཞོང་བསམ་པས། དེ་དང་མ
གོ་བར་འདུག །དུས་སྐྱིགས་མའི་སེམས་ཅན་རྣམས་ལ་ཆོས་མི་ཞོང་བ་
སེམས་ལ་བདུད་ཞུགས་པ་ཡིན་པ་སྐྱིང་རེ་རྗེ་དགོངས་ནས། དབོན་པོ་
གཉིས་ཀྱིས་གཙོས་པའི་བུ་སློབ་ཐམས་ཅད་འཚོགས་ཧོག་གསུངས་པས།
ཐམས་ཅད་ཚོགས་ཞོང་ནས་ང་རྒྱལ་ཞིངས་སེམས་བདུད་ཀྱི་རིགས་རྣམས

145

ལོག་པར་བལྟ་བའི་གཉེན་དེ་རྣམས་ཅེ་ཡིན་གསུངས་ནས་བརྒྱུན་པ་ལ།
དབེན་པོ་དང་བུ་སྒྲུབ་ཐབས་ཅད་ཀྱིས་ཕྱུག་མང་དུ་ཕུལ། ཁྭ་མ་ལ་གསོལ་
བ་བཏབ་པ་དང་། སྨོན་ལམ་གྱི་རྒྱས་འདེབས་བཟང་པོ་ཕུལ་བས། ཁྭ་
མས་འདི་སྐད་གསུངས། ཡང་གཅིག་གསོན་དང་དབོན་རྒྱུང་ང་རྒྱལ་ཅན། །
ང་ཡི་རྣམ་ཐར་ལོ་རྒྱས་ཟབ་མོ་འདིས། །ཉིན་མོ་མི་གྲོལ་མཆན་མོ་ལྟ་འདེ་
གྲོལ། །མི་དང་ལྷ་འདི་གཉིས་པོར་དེ་དག་ཀྱང་། །མི་ལས་ལྷ་འདི་གྲོལ་
ཚན་ཆེ་བར་འོང་། །མི་ཡི་ལུས་འདི་མ་རིག་འཐིབས་པོས་སྒྲིབ། །སེམས་
ལ་ཡིན་མིན་ཁ་ནས་ཅུ་ཚུ་སྒྲོག །མི་དུང་ཐེ་ཚོམ་མི་དགེ་ལྟུ་ཚོགས་འཆར། །
སྐྱེ་བ་གཏན་གྱི་བསོད་ནམས་ཐམས་ཅད་ཟད། །དེ་འདྲའི་དཔུ་ནག་ཚོས་
དེད་ཕྱགས་རྗེས་རྗུངས། །གཙོང་རོང་ཁམས་ཀྱི་མི་ནག་པོ་མོ་ཡིས། །
སངས་རྒྱས་དངོས་སུ་བྱོན་ཀྱང་སྒྲོལ་ཞིག་བཏགས། །བསམ་མི་ཤེས་པས་
གྲུབ་མཐའི་ཕྱོགས་རིས་འཛིན། །ཆགས་སྡང་སྟོང་པས་ཕ་རོལ་ག་ལ་ནོན། །
ཆུར་ལ་རང་ཉིད་ལྷུང་བ་ནག་འཕྲམས་ཕོག །དེ་དག་སྐྱ་སེར་ཡོངས་ཀྱི་མི་
ཤེས་པས། །ཀུན་བྱེད་གྲོངས་ནས་ཟི་ར་དམར་ནག་འཆུབས། །དེ་བཞིན་ཁ་
ནས་མེ་ལྕེ་དམར་པོ་འཕྱིལ། །དེ་ཡི་རྣམ་པར་སྨིན་པ་འདི་བཞིན་འབྱུང་། །
སྐྱད་ཅིག་མེ་ཡི་ཁང་པ་རྗེ་བཞིན་དུ། །ཕྱི་ནི་ས་མདོག་རྗེ་མདོག་རང་བཞིན་
ལ། །ནང་ནི་མེ་དང་དུ་བའི་རང་བཞིན་ནག །རགན་སེར་པོའི་སྲུག་ཕུམ་
རྗེ་བཞིན་དུ། །ཕྱི་སེར་ནང་ནག་བན་དེ་ང་རྒྱལ་ཅན། །ང་རྒྱལ་ཆེན་པོས་
བར་དོ་ཨེ་ཚོད་འོང་། །ཕྱོགས་རིས་མེད་པའི་དག་སྣང་མ་བྱས་པས། །
ཕྱོགས་ལྟེའི་འདོད་གཉེན་དམྱལ་བ་རང་གིས་སྒྲུབ། །འཇིགས་པར་རང་གི་

༄༅། །སེམས་རྒྱུད་མ་བཏུལ་ན། །ཁ་རྒྱངས་ཆོས་གཏམ་ཆགས་སྤང་
ཕྱུང་པོ་ཡིན། །སངས་རྒྱས་བསྟན་པའི་སྒྲུབ་སྟེ་ཆེན་པོ་དང༌། །མཆན་དང་
ལྱན་པའི་བླ་མ་དག་པ་ལ། །མཐོན་སྒྲོག་མེད་པའི་ཞབས་ཕྱི་སྒྲུབ་པ་ནི། །
འདི་ཕྱི་གཉིས་ཡོད་རང་གི་བསོད་ནམས་རྒྱས། །དཔོན་གྱི་ངོ་ཕྱང་མི་གཏོང་
རང་ཕྱུང་ཡིན། །ཉེ་བའི་ངོ་སྲུང་པ་འཁོན་ག་ཤེད་མ་ཡིན། །བླ་རྗེ་དཔོན་
གཡོག་འདི་ཕྱི་སྐྱོང་ཟད་ཡིན། །ཁྲིམ་གྱི་བཟའ་དཔོན་སྐྱིད་སྡུག་སྐྱོས་ཁྱུར་
ཡིན༔ །ད་རེས་མི་ལུས་ལན་གཅིག་ཐོབ་པའི་དུས། །འདི་ཕྱི་སྐྱོང་ཟད་གོར་
ན་གོད་ཆབས་ཆེ། །མ་འོངས་སེམས་ཅན་ཕུགས་ལ་དེ་ལྟར་ཞོག །སྙིང་
གཏམ་མང་ན་ཞེ་ཁྲེལ་འདོག་པའི་རྒྱུ། །ད་ནས་བཟུང་སྟེ་དུས་རྣམས་ཐམས་
ཅད་ལ། །ཕྱོགས་རིས་ཆགས་སྡང་ཀུན་བྲེད་གྱོང་ནས་སྦོངས། །དགའ་སྡུག་
ཕྱོགས་མེད་ཀུན་བྲེད་གྱོང་ནས་སྦོངས། །དགེ་དང་མི་དགེ་ཀུན་བྲེད་གྱོང་
ནས་འབྱུང༌། །ད་ལྟའི་དུས་ཀྱི་གྲུབ་མཐའ་བཟང་ངན་འདི། །བཟང་པོ་
གང་ཡིན་ངན་པ་གང་ཡིན་ལ། །ཀུན་བྲེད་རྒྱལ་པོའི་གྱོང་ནས་བཟང་ངན་
འབྱུང༔ །དགར་པོའི་དགེ་བ་གྱུང་ན་ཉམས་རེ་མཆར། །ཉག་པོའི་སྡིག
པ་བྱུང་ན་ཡི་རེ་མུག །སྐྱེ་བ་མང་པོ་འཛོམ་གྱི་ཡུལ་དུ་བྱུངས། །ཆོས་
ལུགས་བཞི་ལ་མ་བཀུར་གང་ཡང་མེད། །ཆོས་སྒོ་བཞི་ལ་མ་ཞུགས་གང་
ཡང་མེད། །བཟང་པོ་འདི་ཡིན་ངན་པ་འདི་ཡིན་ཞེས། །བཟང་ངན་དབྱེ་བ
ང་ལ་མ་བྱུང་བས། །ཆོས་རྣམས་ཐམས་ཅད་སངས་རྒྱས་ཡུལ་དུ་གཅིག །
བྱུང་བ་སངས་རྒྱས་རྣམས་ཀྱི་ཕྱགས་ལས་བྱུང༌། །ཕྱགས་ལས་བྱུང་ཞིང་ཞལ
ནས་གསུངས་པའི་ཆོས། །གཅིག་ལ་བཟང་བའི་ཆོས་ཤིག་གསུངས་པ

༄༅། །དང༌། །ཤེ་པའི་ཚོགས་ཤིག་ག་ཅིག་ལ་གནང་བ་མིན། །སངས་
རྒྱས་ཡུལ་ནས་བཟང་དང་མ་བྱུང་ཡང༌། །མ་རིག་ཡུལ་ནས་བཟང་པོ་ངན་པ་
བྱུང༌། །ང་ཡིས་སྐྱེ་བ་མང་པོ་བཀྱུད་པ་ལས། །ཁྱག་ཆེན་ལམ་འབྲས་དབུ་
མ་ལྷ་ལྷུན་དང༌། །བཀའ་གདམས་རྫོགས་པ་ཆེན་པོ་ལ་སོགས་པའི། །
ཚོས་ཡུགས་གྲུབ་མཐའ་སོ་སོའི་འགྲོ་དོན་ནི། །ཐམས་ཅད་ང་ཡིས་མ་
བསླབས་གང་ཡང་མེད། །དེ་ཕྱིར་རང་ལ་གྲུབ་མཐའ་ཕྱོགས་རིས་མེད། །
ཕྱོགས་རིས་ཆགས་སྡང་སྤངས་པས་རང་སར་གྲོལ། །མ་ཉིངས་ཕྱི་རབས་
རྗེས་འཇུག་བུ་སློབ་རྣམས། །ཕྱོགས་རིས་སྟོངས་ལ་དགའ་སྡང་ཕྱོགས་མེད་
སྟོངས༔ །སྐྱབས་གནས་བསྒུ་མེད་ཡིན་ནོ་ཡིན་ལ་ཟོག །ཅེས་གསུངས་
པས༔ དབོན་པོ་དགེ་འདུན་རྒྱ་མཚོ་སོགས་འདུས་པ་ཐམས་ཅད་ཀྱིས་ཡུག་
མང་དུ་འཚལ་ནས། བླ་མ་ཁྱེད་ཀྱིས་ཞལ་གདམས་དང་སྐྱེས་རབས་རྟེན་གྱི་
ལོ་རྒྱུས་ཞལ་ཆེམས་དང་བཅས་པ་ཕྱགས་རྗེ་ཆེའོ། །དེ་ནི་འགྲོ་བ་མི་དང་མི་
མ་ཡིན་ལ་སོགས་པའི་སྐྱེ་འགྲོ་དབུགས་ཕོབ་ཆད་དང༌། །འབས་གསུམ་སྒྱིང་
བཞིའི་སེམས་ཅན་ཐམས་ཅད་སངས་རྒྱས་ཀྱི་ས་ལ་འགོད་ནས་པའི་ཚོས་ཀྱི་
ཆར་འབེབས་པར་གྱུར་ཅིག །འབྱོར་བ་དང་དང་སོང་གི་སྲུག་བསྲལ་རྒྱ་
མཚོ་ཆེན་པོ་ལས་ཐར་བར་གྱུར་ཅིག །མ་གྱུར་འགྲོ་བ་མཁའ་ཁྱབ་ཀྱི་
སེམས་ཅན་ཐམས་ཅད་བླ་ན་མེད་པ་སངས་རྒྱས་ཀྱི་གོ་འཕང་མཆོག་གྱུར་དུ་
ཐོབ་པར་གྱུར་ཅིག་ཅེས་སྨོན་ལམ་བཏབ་བོ། དེ་ལྟར་སྐྱེ་དྲན་ཉི་མ་བཀྲ་
ཤིས་ཀྱི་སྐྱེས་རབས་རྟེན་གྱི་ལོ་རྒྱུས་ཞལ་ཆེམས་དང་བཅུས་པ་རྫོགས་སོ།།
འདིར་སྨྲས་པ། ཨེ་མ། ཡང་དག་ཟབ་མོའི་ཚོས་སྒོ་མ་ལུས་པ། །

148

༄༅། །སློན་མཛད་བླ་མ་མཆོག་གི་གསུང་རྗེ་སྟེད། །མ་བསྐུད་བུང་
བས་པད་ཆལ་བཅུད་བསྲུས་འདི། །བསྐུན་འགྲོ་ཡོངས་ལ་ཁན་བདེའི་རྒྱར་
གྱུར་ཅིག །དེ་ཡང་དཔལ་ལྡན་བླ་མ་དམ་པའི་གསུངས་མགུར་ཞལ་
གདམས་སྐྱེ་བ་དྲན་པའི་རྣམ་ཐར་རྟེན་གྱི་དགར་ཆག་དང་བཅས་པ་འདི་
རྣམས༔     དཔེ་ཆ་མང་དུག་པས་གོང་འོག་གི་གནས་འཚོལ་བ་རྣམས་
མཐའ་གཅིག་ཏུ་མ་ངེས་ཤིང་། ཤེ་ཚོམ་གྱི་གནས་སུ་འདུག་པ་རྣམས་སྟོན་གྱི་
ཡིག་སྙིང་དག་པ་རྣམས་ལས་ལེགས་པ་གཤིགས་ཏེ་ཁྲིགས་སུ་བསྟེབས་པར་
གྱིས་ཤེས་རྗེ་བཅུན་མཁྱེན་བརྗེའི་བདག་ཉིད་སྒྲུབ་བརྒྱུད་བསྟན་འཛིན་ཡེ་
ཤེས་ཏེ་མ་ཕྱིན་ལས་མཆོག་ཏུ་རྒྱས་པའི་སྲེས་བགའ་སྐྱལ་སྒྲི་བོར་ཕེབས་པ་
ལས་རྗེ་བཞིན་རྟོགས་པའི་སྒྲོབས་པ་དང་མི་ལྡན་ཀྱང་། །    འབད་པས་དང་
དུ་བླངས་ཏེ་མཛེས་ཚོས་དང་བསྒྱད་པའི་ཚིག་རྒྱུན་སོགས་བཙོས་བསྣུད་ཀྱི་དི་
མ་དང་བྲལ་བ་འདི་ལྟ་བུ་བགྱིས་པ་པོ་རྗེ་བཅུན་དམ་པ་འདི་ཡིས་སྐྱེ་དང་ཚེ་
རབས་ཀུན་ཏུ་རྗེས་སུ་བཟུང་བ་བགའ་འབངས་ཐ་ཤལ་བ་མིང་སྣྲ་རྒྱ་དར་
འབོད་པ་བདག་རང་བློ་སུམ་ཚུས་འབྱུག་ལོ་ཏོར་རྣ་བཅུ་གཉིས་པའི་ཚེས་
བཟང་པོ་ལ་གྲུབ་པའི་གནས་མཆོག་དཔལ་ལྡན་བགྲ་ཤིས་ཚོས་གྱིང་དུ་
བགོད་པ་འདིས་ཀྱང་བསྐུན་དང་འགྲོ་བའི་དོན་ཆེན་ལྷུན་གྱུབ་ཏུ་འབྱུང་བར་
གྱུར་ཅིག །མངྒ་ལྂ་བྷ་ཝནྟུ། །དགེའོ།།

༄༅། །སྐྱི་དབན་ཉི་མ་བཀྲ་ཤིས་ཀྱི་སྐུ་ཕྲེང་རིམ་བྱོན་ལ་
གསོལ་འདེབས་བྱིན་རློབས་ཆར་འབེབས་བཞུགས་སོ།།

༄༅། །སྐྱེ་དགུན་ཉི་མ་བདག་ཉིས་ཀྱི་སྐུ་ཕྱིང་རིམ་བྱིན་ལ་གསོལ་འདེབས་
བྱིན་རློབས་ཆར་འབེབས་བཞུགས་སོ།། དགོན་མཆོག་གསུམ་གྱི་གསང་
གསུམ་འདུས་པའི་བདག །གསང་བའི་བདག་པོ་དཔལ་ལྡན་རྡོ་རྗེ་འཛིན། །
མཐའ་ཡས་ཡིན་ལས་ཕྱིན་ལས་རྒྱ་མཚོའི་རོལ་གར་ལས། །གཉིས་སུ་མེད་པའི་
བདག་ཉིད་གསོལ་བ་འདེབས། །རིག་འཛིན་ཕོགས་མེད་འོད་ལྷན་གྲུབ་
པའི་དཔལ། །སྐྱལ་པའི་སྣང་སྟོན་དག་པ་ཞེས་རབ་ཞབས། །ཕྱགས་རྗེའི་
གཏེར་མངའ་འགྲོ་མགོན་ལོ་ཙཱ་བ། །ས་བཅུའི་དབང་ཕྱུག་གསུམ་ལ་གསོལ་
བ་འདེབས། །ཚེས་སྨྲ་རྡོ་རྗེ་བསྐྱེད་རྫོགས་གདམས་པའི་མཛོད། །འཛར་
ལུས་མཆོག་བརྙེས་རྡོ་རྗེ་གྲགས་པ་དང་། །བླ་མེད་གྲུབ་པ་བརྙེས་པའི་
གསལ་སྟོང་བ། །གྲུབ་པའི་དབང་ཕྱུག་གསུམ་ལ་གསོལ་བ་འདེབས། །

153

པ་ཙ་ཆེན་དགག་གི་དབང་ཕྱུག་འགྲོ་བའི་མགོན། །ཀྱེ་རྗེ་ཐེག་པའི་མཆོང་
འཛིན་ཁྲག་སྐྱག་དང་། །ས་གསུམ་འགྲན་ཟླ་དྲེལ་སྤུ་རའི་ཞབས། །
བསྟན་པའི་མངའ་བདག་གསུམ་ལ་གསོལ་བ་འདེབས། །རྒྱལ་བསྟན་སྤེལ་
མཛད་ཚོས་དབང་དཔལ་བཟང་པོ། །སངས་རྒྱས་བསྟན་འཛིན་འགྲོ་དོན་
ཕྱིན་ལས་བདག །གྲུབ་གཉིས་མངའ་བ་བསོད་ནམས་བཀྲ་ཤིས་ཞེས། །
ཕྱིན་ལས་དབང་བསྐྱར་གསུམ་ལ་གསོལ་བ་འདེབས། །དགའ་གི་དབང་ཕྱུག
ཤེས་རབ་རྒྱ་མཚོ་དང་། །འགྲོ་བའི་མགོན་པོ་ཀུན་དགའ་བསོད་ནམས
མཚན། །བསྒྱུ་མེད་སྐྱབས་གཅིག་བཀྲ་ཤིས་དོན་ཀུན་གྲུབ། །ཐར་པའི
ལམ་སྟོན་གསུམ་ལ་གསོལ་བ་འདེབས། །ཚོས་ཀྱི་རྒྱལ་པོ་ཉི་མ་བཀྲ་ཤེས
དང་། །ས་སྐྱོང་གཙུག་རྒྱན་ཉི་མ་འགྱུར་མེད་པ། །གྲུབ་དབང་ཉི་མ་བསྟན
པའི་གསལ་བྱེད་མཚོག །སྐུ་བས་གནས་མཚུངས་མེད་གསུམ་ལ་གསོལ་བ
འདེབས། །བདེ་སྟོང་མཚོག་བརྗེས་ཚོས་རྒྱལ་དབང་པོའི་སྲེ། །ཀྱེ་རྗེ་འཛིན
དངོས་ཕྱིན་ལས་ཉི་མ་དང་། །ཡེ་ཤེས་སྣང་བའི་མཚོག་སྤྲིན་ཉི་མ་ཆེ། །
ཕྱགས་རྗེའི་གདུར་མངའ་གསུམ་ལ་གསོལ་བ་འདེབས། །བསྒྲུབ་ལ་གསུམ
གྱིས་རབ་བརྒྱན་དཔེར་འོས་པ། །གྲུབ་པའི་མཐར་སོན་སྲས་པའི་རྩལ
འབྱོར་ཆེ། །བསྟན་འགྲོའི་དཔལ་མངའ་རྩ་མེད་རྡོ་རྗེ་འཆང་། །ཀུན་ཁྱབ
ཉི་མའི་ཞབས་ལ་གསོལ་བ་འདེབས། །སྲིགས་མའི་མགོན་ཀྱུར་རྡོ་རྗེ་འཛིན
པ་ཉིད། །འགྲོ་བའི་དོན་དུ་སྤྲིན་པའི་སྐུར་སྣང་བའི། །དཔལ་ལྡན་བླ་མ
མཚོག་གི་སྐྱེས་རབས་ཕྲེང་། །རིམ་པར་བྱིན་པ་རྣམས་ལ་གསོལ་བ
འདེབས། །དེ་ལྟར་རྗེ་བཙུན་བླ་མར་གསོལ་བཏབ་མཐུས། །མགོན་པོ

༄༅། །མཆོག་གིས་རྗེས་སུ་འཛིན་པ་དང་། །ཕྱུག་ལམ་རྟོགས་དང་དབུ་
མ་ཞི་བྱེད་གཞུང་། །སོ་སོའི་དོན་ལ་མ་རྟོངས་རིམ་གཞིས་ཀྱི། །ལམ་ལ་
འཇུག་ནས་མཆོན་རྟོགས་སངས་རྒྱས་ཕོག །སྐྱེ་ཞིང་སྐྱེ་བ་དག་ནི་ཐམས་
ཅད་དུ། །རིགས་བཟང་བློ་གསལ་ང་རྒྱལ་མེད་པ་དང་། །སྙིང་རྗེ་ཆེ་ཞིང་བླ་
མ་ལ་གུས་ལྡན། །དཔལ་ལྡན་བླ་མའི་དམ་ཚིག་ལ་གནས་ཤོག །དཔལ་
ལྡན་བླ་མའི་རྣམ་པར་ཐར་པ་ལ། །སྐད་ཅིག་ཙམ་ཡང་ལོག་ལྟ་མི་སྐྱེ་ཞིང་། །
ཅི་མཛད་ལེགས་པར་མཐོང་བའི་མོས་གུས་ཀྱིས། །བླ་མའི་བྱིན་རླབས་
སེམས་ལ་འཇུག་པར་ཤོག །སྐྱེ་བ་ཀུན་ཏུ་ཡང་དག་བླ་མ་དང་། །འབྲལ་
མེད་ཆོས་ཀྱི་དཔལ་ལ་ལོངས་སྤྱོད་ཅིང་། །ས་དང་ལམ་གྱི་ཡོན་ཏན་རབ་
རྟོགས་ནས། །རྡོ་རྗེ་འཆང་གི་གོ་འཕང་མྱུར་ཐོབ་ཤོག །ཅེས་པའང་སྟུ་
བླ་དུའི་མིང་འཛིན་པ་བདག་གིས། །ཆུ་བའི་བླ་མ་རིམ་བྱོན་རྣམས་ལ་དད་
པའི་ཡིད་ཀྱིས་གསོལ་བ་བཏབ་པའོ།། །། ཤུ་བྷཾ།།

# Acknowledgments

We would like to express our gratitude to the Ninth Traleg Kyabgön Rinpoche for his blessing, to Khenpo Karthar Rinpoche for his guidance and encouragement, and to Lama Karma Drodül for inputting the Tibetan text and for answering all our questions.

We also express our appreciation to our invaluable assistant Jigme Nyima, to Naomi Schmidt for her guidance and technical assistance, to Sally Clay for her professional assistance, to Dee Collings and Michael Erlewine for the photographs of Traleg Rinpoche, and to all those at E-Vam Institute, Karme Ling, and KTD who offered their support.

*Yeshe Gyamtso, Maureen McNicholas, and*
*Peter van Deurzen—KTD Publications*

The Ninth Traleg Kyabgön Rinpoche
E-Vam Institute, Chatham, New York, 2006

# E-Vam Institute

Traleg Rinpoche's centers are devoted specifically to preserving the pristine and authentic traditional teachings, which were designed to stimulate and transform the mind.

Kagyu E-Vam Buddhist Institute
673 Lygon Street
Carlton North, Vic, 3054
Australia
Phone: (61 3) 9387 0422
Email: e_vam@smartchat.net.au
Web: www.evaminstitute.org.au

E-Vam Buddhist Institute
171 Water Street
Chatham, NY 12037
Phone: 518-392-6900
E-mail: office@evam.org
Web: www.evam.org

Nyima Tashi Kagyu Buddhist Centre
20 Williamson Avenue
Grey Lynn
Auckland, NZ
Phone: 64-9-361-2305
E-mail: nyimatashi.nz@gmail.com
Web: www.nyima-tashi.org.nz

# Karma Triyana Dharmachakra

Karma Triyana Dharmachakra (KTD) is the North America seat of His Holiness the Gyalwa Karmapa, and under the spiritual guidance and protection of His Holiness Ogyen Trinley Dorje, the Seventeenth Gyalwa Karmapa, is devoted to the authentic representation of the Kagyu lineage of Tibetan Buddhism.

For information regarding KTD, including our current schedule, or for information regarding our affiliate centers, Karma Thegsum Choling (KTC), located both in the United States and internationally, contact us using the information below.

Karma Triyana Dharmachakra
335 Meads Mountain Road
Woodstock, NY, 12498 USA
845 679 5906 ext. 10
www.kagyu.org
KTC Coordinator: 845 679 5701
ktc@kagyu.org

160

# KTD Publications

GATHERING THE GARLANDS OF THE GURUS' PRECIOUS TEACHINGS

KTD Publications, a part of Karma Triyana Dharmachakra, is a not-for-profit publisher established with the purpose of facilitating the projects and activities manifesting from His Holiness's inspiration and blessings. We are dedicated to gathering the garlands of precious teachings and producing fine-quality books.

We invite you to join KTD Publications in facilitating the activities of His Holiness Karmapa and fulfilling the wishes of Khenpo Karthar Rinpoche and Bardor Tulku Rinpoche. If you would like to sponsor a book or make a donation to KTD Publications, please contact us using the information below. All contributions are tax-deductible.

KTD Publications
335 Meads Mountain Road
Woodstock, NY, 12498 USA
Telephone: 845 679 5906 ext. 37
www.KTDPublications.org

# Also from KTD Publications

*Karma Chakme's Mountain Dharma as Taught by Khenpo Karthar Rinpoche, Volume One*, 2005

*Karma Chakme's Mountain Dharma as Taught by Khenpo Karthar Rinpoche, Volume Two*, 2006

*Karma Chakme's Mountain Dharma as Taught by Khenpo Karthar Rinpoche, Volumes Three, Four, and Five*, 2007-2008

*Precious Essence: The Inner Autobiography of Terchen Barway Dorje*, Foreword by His Holiness the Seventeenth Karmapa, Ogyen Trinley Dorje, translated by Yeshe Gyamtso, 2005

*The Vajra Garland & The Lotus Garden: Treasure Biographies of Padmakara and Vairochana*, by Jamgön Kongtrul Lodrö Taye, Foreword by the Fourth Jamgön Kongtrul Rinpoche, Lodrö Chökyi Nyima, translated by Yeshe Gyamtso, 2005

*Chariot of the Fortunate: The Life of the First Yongey Mingyur Dorje Rinpoche* by Je Tukyi Dorje & Surmang Tendzin Rinpoche, Foreword by the Seventh Yongey Mingyur Dorje, translated by Yeshe Gyamtso, English and Tibetan, 2006